PARSONS. DEL. AVERY. SC.

ASTORIA, AS IT WAS IN 1813.

NARRATIVE

OF A

VOYAGE

TO

THE NORTHWEST COAST OF AMERICA

IN THE YEARS 1811, 1812, 1813, AND 1814

OR THE

FIRST AMERICAN SETTLEMENT ON THE PACIFIC

By GABRIEL FRANCHERE

TRANSLATED AND EDITED BY J. V. HUNTINGTON

REDFIELD
110 AND 112 NASSAU STREET, NEW YORK
1854.

Entered, according to Act of Congress, in the year 1854,

By J. S. REDFIELD,

in the Clerk's Office of the District Court of the United States, in and for the Southern District of New York.

STEREOTYPED BY C. C. SAVAGE,
13 Chambers Street, N. Y.

PREFACE TO THE SECOND EDITION.

In 1846, when the boundary question (that of the Oregon Territory in particular) was at its height, the Hon. Thomas H. Benton delivered in the United States Senate a decisive speech, of which the following is an extract:—

"Now for the proof of all I have said. I happen to have in my possession the book of all others, which gives the fullest and most authentic details on all the points I have mentioned—a book written at a time, and under circumstances, when the author (himself a British subject and familiar on the Columbia) had no more idea that the British would lay claim to that river, than

Mr. Harmon, the American writer whom I quoted, ever thought of our claiming New Caledonia. It is the work of Mr. FRANCHERE, a gentleman of Montreal, with whom I have the pleasure to be personally acquainted, and one of those employed by Mr. ASTOR in founding his colony. He was at the founding of ASTORIA, at its sale to the Northwest Company, saw the place seized as a British conquest, and continued there after its seizure. He wrote in French: his work has not been done into English, though it well deserves it; and I read from the French text. He gives a brief and true account of the discovery of the Columbia."

I felt justly proud of this notice of my unpretending work, especially that the latter should have contributed, as it did, to the amicable settlement of the then pending difficulties. I have flattered myself ever since, that it belonged to the historical literature of the great country, which by adoption has become mine.

The re-perusal of "Astoria" by WASHINGTON IRVING (1836) inspired me with an additional motive for giving my book in an English dress. Without disparagement to Mr. IRVING'S literary fame, I may venture to say that I found in his work inaccuracies, misstatements (unintentional of course), and a want of chronological order, which struck forcibly one so familiar with the events themselves. I thought I could show—or rather that my simple narration, of itself, plainly discovered—that some of the young men embarked in that expedition (which founded our Pacific empire), did not merit the ridicule and contempt which Captain THORN attempted to throw upon them, and which perhaps, through the genius of Mr. IRVING, might otherwise remain as a lasting stigma on their characters.

But the consideration which, before all others, prompts me to offer this narrative to the American reading public, is my desire to place before them, therein, a simple and connected account (which at this time ought to be interesting), of the early settlement of the Oregon Territory by one of our adopted citizens, the enterprising merchant JOHN JACOB ASTOR. The importance of a vast territory, which at no distant day may add two more bright stars to our national banner, is a guarantee that my humble effort will be appreciated.

NOTE BY THE EDITOR.

It has been the editor's wish to let Mr. Franchere speak for himself. To preserve in the translation the Defoe-like simplicity of the original narrative of the young French Canadian, has been his chief care. Having read many narratives of travel and adventure in our northwestern wilderness, he may be permitted to say that he has met with none that gives a more vivid and picturesque description of it, or in which the personal adventures of the narrator, and the varying fortunes of a great enterprise, mingle more happily, and one may say, more dramatically, with the itinerary. The clerkly minuteness of the details is not without its charm either, and their fidelity speaks for itself. Take it altogether, it must be regarded as a fragment of our colonial history saved from oblivion; it fills up a vacuity which Mr. IRVING'S classic work does not quite supply; it is, in fact, the only account by an eye-witness and a participator in the enterprise, of the first attempt to form a settlement on the Pacific under the stars and stripes.

The editor has thought it would be interesting to add Mr. Franchere's Preface to the original French edition, which will be found on the next page.

BALTIMORE, *February* 6, 1854.

PREFACE TO THE FRENCH EDITION.

WHEN I was writing my journal on the vessel which carried me to the northwest coast of North America, or in the wild regions of this continent, I was far from thinking that it would be placed one day before the public eye. I had no other end in writing, but to procure to my family and my friends a more exact and more connected detail of what I had seen or learned in the course of my travels, than it would have been possible for me to give them in a *viva voce* narration. Since my return to my native city, my manuscript has passed into various hands and has been read by different persons: several of my friends immediately advised me to print it; but it is only quite lately that I have allowed myself to be persuaded, that without being a learned naturalist, a skilful geographer, or a profound moralist, a traveller may yet interest by the faithful and succinct account of the situations in which he has found himself, the adventures which have happened to him, and the incidents of which he has been a witness; that if a simple ingenuous narrative, stripped of the merit of science and the graces of diction, must needs be less enjoyed by the man of letters or by the *savant*, it would have, in compensation, the advantage of being at the level of a greater number of readers; in fine, that the desire of affording an entertainment to his countrymen, according to his capacity, and without any mixture of the author's vanity or of pecuniary interest, would be a well-founded title to their indulgence. Whether I have done well or ill in yielding to these suggestions, which I am bound to regard as those of friendship, or of good-will, it belongs to the impartial and disinterested reader to decide.

MONTREAL, 1819.

CONTENTS.

CHAPTER V.

CHAPTER VI.

CHAPTER VII.

CHAPTER VIII.

CHAPTER IX.

CHAPTER X.

CHAPTER XI.

CHAPTER XII.

CHAPTER XIII.

CHAPTER XIV.

CHAPTER XV.

CHAPTER XXVII.

CHAPTER XXVIII.

CHAPTER XXIX.

APPENDIX.

INTRODUCTION.

Since the independence of the United States of America, the merchants of that industrious and enterprising nation have carried on an extremely advantageous commerce on the north-west coast of this continent. In the course of their voyages they have made a great number of discoveries which they have not thought proper to make public; no doubt to avoid competition in a lucrative business.

In 1792, Captain Gray, commanding the ship Columbia of Boston, discovered in latitude 46° 19′ north, the entrance of a great bay on the Pacific coast. He sailed into it, and having perceived that it was the outlet or estuary of a large river, by the fresh water which he found at a little distance from the entrance, he continued his course upward some eighteen miles, and dropped anchor on the left bank, at the opening of a deep bay. There he made a map or rough sketch of what he had seen of this river (accompanied by a written description of the soundings, bearings, &c.); and having finished his traffic with the natives (the object of his voyage to these parts), he put out to sea, and soon after fell in with Captain Vancouver, who was cruising by order of the British government, to seek new discoveries. Mr. Gray acquainted him with the one he had just made, and even gave him a copy of the chart he had drawn up. Vancouver, who had just driven off a colony of Spaniards established on the coast, under the command of Señor Quadra (England and Spain being then at war), despatched his first-lieutenant Broughton, who ascended the river in boats some one hundred and twenty or one hundred and fifty miles, took possession of the country in the name of his Britannic majesty, giving the river the name of the *Columbia*, and to the bay where the American captain stopped, that of *Gray's bay*. Since that period the country had been seldom visited (till 1811), and chiefly by American ships.

Sir Alexander M'Kenzie, in his second overland voyage, tried to reach the western ocean by the Columbia river, and thought he had succeeded when he came out six degrees farther north, at the bottom of Puget's sound, by another river.*

In 1805, the American government sent Captains Lewis and Clark, with about thirty men, including some Kentucky hunters, on an overland journey to the mouth of the Columbia. They ascended the Missouri, crossed the mountains at the source of that river, and following the course of the Columbia, reached the shores of the Pacific, where they were forced to winter. The report which they made of their expedition to the United States government created a lively sensation.†

* M'Kenzie's Travels.

† Lewis and Clark's Report.

Mr. John Jacob Astor, a New York merchant, who conducted almost alone the trade in furs south of the great lakes Huron and Superior, and who had acquired by that commerce a prodigious fortune, thought to augment it by forming on the banks of the Columbia an establishment of which the principal or supply factory should be at the mouth of that river. He communicated his views to the agents of the Northwest Company; he was even desirous of forming the proposed establishment in concert with them; but after some negotiations, the inland or wintering partners of that association of fur-traders having rejected the plan, Mr. Astor determined to make the attempt alone. He needed for the success of his enterprise, men long versed in the Indian trade, and he soon found them. Mr. Alexander M'Kay (the same who had accompanied Sir Alexander M'Kenzie in his travels overland), a bold and enterprising man, left the Northwest Company to join him; and soon after, Messrs Duncan M'Dougal and Donald M'Kenzie (also in the service of the company), and

Messrs. David Stuart and Robert Stuart, all of Canada, did the same. At length, in the winter of 1810, a Mr. Wilson Price Hunt of St. Louis, on the Mississippi, having also joined them, they determined that the expedition should be set on foot in the following spring.

It was in the course of that winter that one of my friends made me acquainted in confidence with the plan of these gentlemen, under the injunction of strictest secrecy. The desire of seeing strange countries, joined to that of acquiring a fortune, determined me to solicit employment of the new association; on the 20th of May I had an interview with Mr. A. M'Kay, with whom the preliminaries were arranged; and on the 24th of the same month I signed an agreement as an apprenticed clerk for the term of five years.

When the associates had engaged a sufficient number of Canadian boatmen, they equipped a bark canoe under charge of Messrs. Hunt and M'Kenzie, with a Mr. Perrault as clerk, and a crew of fourteen men. These gentlemen were to proceed to Mackinaw, and thence to St. Louis, hiring on the way as many men as they could to man the canoes, in which, from the last-mentioned port, they were to ascend the Missouri to its source, and there diverging from the route followed by Lewis and Clark, reach the mouth of the Columbia to form a junction with another party, who were to go round by way of Cape Horn. In the course of my narrative I shall have occasion to speak of the success of both these expeditions.

NARRATIVE OF A VOYAGE

TO THE

NORTHWEST COAST OF AMERICA.

CHAPTER I.

Departure from Montreal.—Arrival in New York.—Description of that City.—Names of the Persons engaged in the Expedition.

WE remained in Montreal the rest of the spring and a part of the summer. At last, having completed our arrangements for the journey, we received orders to proceed, and on the 26th of July, accompanied by my father and brothers and a few friends, I repaired to the place of embarkation, where was prepared a birch bark canoe, manned by nine Canadians, having Mr. A. M'Kay as commander, and a Mr. A. Fisher as passenger. The sentiments which I experienced at that moment would be as difficult for me to describe as they were painful to support; for the first time in my life I quitted the place of my birth, and was separated from beloved parents and intimate friends, having for my whole consolation the faint hope of seeing them again. We embarked at about five, P. M., and arrived at La Prairie de la Madeleine (on the opposite side of the St. Lawrence), toward eight o'clock.* We slept at this village, and the next morning, very early, having secured the canoe on a wagon, we got in motion again, and reached St. John's on the river Richelieu, a little before noon. Here we relaunched our canoe (after having well calked the seams), crossed or rather traversed the length of Lake Champlain, and arrived at Whitehall on the 30th. There we were overtaken by Mr. Ovid de Montigny, and a Mr. P. D. Jeremie, who were to be of the expedition.

Having again placed our canoe on a wagon,

* This place is famous in the history of Canada, and more particularly in the thrilling story of the Indian missions.—ED.

we pursued our journey, and arrived on the 1st of August at Lansingburg, a little village situated on the bank of the river Hudson. Here we got our canoe once more afloat, passed by Troy, and by Albany, everywhere hospitably received, our Canadian boatmen, having their hats decorated with parti-colored ribands and feathers, being taken by the Americans for so many wild Indians, and arrived at New York on the 3d, at eleven o'clock in the evening.

We had landed at the north end of the city, and the next day, being Sunday, we re-embarked, and were obliged to make a course round the city, in order to arrive at our lodgings on Long Island. We sang as we rowed; which, joined to the unusual sight of a birch bark canoe impelled by nine stout Canadians, dark as Indians, and as gayly adorned, attracted a crowd upon the wharves to gaze at us as we glided along. We found on Long Island (in the village of Brooklyn) those young gentlemen engaged in the service of the new company, who had left Canada in advance of our party.

The vessel in which we were to sail not being ready, I should have found myself quite isolated and a stranger in the great city of New York, but for a letter of introduction to Mr. G——, given me on my setting out, by Madame his sister. I had formed the acquaintance of this gentleman during a stay which he had made at Montreal in 1801; but as I was then very young, he would probably have had some difficulty in recognising me without his sister's letter. He introduced me to several of his friends, and I passed in an agreeable manner the five weeks which elapsed between my arrival in New York and the departure of the ship.

I shall not undertake to describe New York; I will only say, that the elegance of the buildings, public and private, the cleanliness of the streets, the shade of the poplars which border them, the public walks, the markets always abundantly provided with all sorts of commodities, the activity of its commerce, then in a flourishing condition, the vast number of ships of all nations which crowded the quays; all, in a word, conspired to make me feel the difference between this great maritime city and my native town, of whose steeples I had never lost sight before, and which was by no means at that time what it is now.

New York was not then, and indeed is not at this time a fortified town; still there were several batteries and military works, the most considerable of which were seen on the *Narrows*, or channel which forms the principal mouth of the Hudson. The isles called *Governor's Island*, and *Bedloe* or *Gibbet Island*, were also well fortified. On the first, situated to the west of the city and about a mile from it, there were barracks sufficiently capacious for several thousand soldiers, and a Moro, or castle, with three tiers of guns, all bomb-proof. These works have been strengthened during the last war.

The market-places are eight in number; the most considerable is called *Fly-Market*.

The *Park*, the *Battery*, and *Vauxhall Garden*, are the principal promenades. There were, in 1810, thirty-two churches, two of which were devoted to the catholic worship; and the population was estimated at ninety thousand souls, of whom ten thousand were French. It is thought that this population has since been augmented (1819) by some thirty thousand souls.

During my sojourn at New York, I lodged in Brooklyn, on Long Island. This island is separated from the city by a sound, or narrow arm of the sea. There is here a pretty village, not far from which is a basin, where some gun-boats were hauled up, and a few war vessels were on the stocks. Some barracks had been constructed here, and a guard was maintained.

Before leaving New York, it is well to observe that during our stay in that city, Mr. M'Kay thought it the part of prudence to have an interview with the minister plenipotentiary of his Britannic majesty, Mr. Jackson,* to inform him of the object of our voyage, and get his views in regard to the line of conduct we ought to follow in case of war breaking out between the two powers; intimating to him that we were all Brit-

* This gentleman was really *chargé d'affaires.*

ish subjects, and were about to trade under the American flag. After some moments of reflection Mr. Jackson told him, "that we were going on a very hazardous enterprise; that he saw our object was purely commercial, and that all he could promise us, was, that in case of a war we should be respected as British subjects and traders."

This reply appeared satisfactory, and Mr. M'Kay thought we had nothing to apprehend on that side.

The vessel in which we were to sail was called the *Tonquin*, of about 300 tons burden, commanded by Captain Thorn (a first-lieutenant of the American navy, on furlough for this purpose), with a crew of twenty-one men. The number of passengers was thirty-three. Here follow the names of both.

PASSENGERS.

PARTNERS	Messrs. Alexander M'Kay	all of Canada.
	" Duncan M'Dougall,	
	" David Stuart,	
	" Robert Stuart,	

CLERKS:

James Lewis of New York.
Russel Farnham of Massachusetts.
William W. Matthews of New York.
Alexander Ross,
Donald M'Gîllis,
Ovide de Montigny,
Francis B. Pillot,
Donald M'Lennan,
William Wallace,
Thomas M'Kay,
Gabriel Franchere, — all from Canada.

BOATMEN, ETC.:

Oliver Roy Lapensée,	Joseph Lapierre,
Ignace Lapensée	Joseph Nadeau,
Basile Lapensée.	J. B'te. Belleau,
Jacques Lafantaisie,	Antoine Belleau,
Benjamin Roussel,	Louis Bruslé,
Michel Laframboise,	P. D. Jeremie,
Giles Leclerc,	all of Canada.

Johann Koaster, ship-carpenter, a Russian,
George Bell, cooper, New York,
Job Aitken, rigger and calker, from Scotland,
Augustus Roussil, blacksmith, Canada,
Guilleaume Perreault, a boy. These last were all mechanics, &c., destined for the establishment.

CREW.

Jonathan Thorn, captain, New York State.
Ebenezer D. Fox, 1st mate, of Boston.
John M. Mumford, 2d mate, of Massachusetts.
James Thorn, brother of the captain, New York.
John Anderson, boatswain, foreigner.
Egbert Vanderhuff, tailor, New York.
John Weeks, carpenter, "

Stephen Weeks, armorer, New York.

John Coles, New York, }
John Martin, a Frenchman, } sailmakers.

SAILORS.
- John White, New York.
- Adam Fisher, "
- Peter Verbel, "
- Edward Aymes, "
- Robert Hill, Albany, New York.
- John Adams, "
- Joseph Johnson, Englishman,
- Charles Roberts, New York,

A colored man as cook,

A mulatto steward,

And three or four others whose names I have forgotten.

CHAPTER II.

Departure from New York.—Reflections of the Author.—Navigation, falling in with other Ships, and various Incidents, till the Vessel comes in Sight of the Falkland Isles.

All being ready for our departure, we went on board ship, and weighed anchor on the 6th of September, in the morning. The wind soon fell off, and the first day was spent in drifting down to Staten island, where we came to anchor for the night. The next day we weighed anchor again; but there came on another dead calm, and we were forced to cast anchor near the light-house at Sandy Hook. On the 8th we weighed anchor for the third time, and by the help of a fresh breeze from the southwest, we succeeded in passing the bar; the pilot quitted us at about eleven o'clock, and soon after we lost sight of the coast.

One must have experienced it one's self, to be able to conceive the melancholy which takes possession of the soul of a man of sensibility, at the instant that he leaves his country and the civilized world, to go to inhabit with strangers in wild and unknown lands. I should in vain endeavor to give my readers an idea, even faintly correct, of the painful sinking of heart that I suddenly felt, and of the sad glance which I involuntarily cast toward a future so much the more frightful to me, as it offered nothing but what was perfectly confused and uncertain. A new scene of life was unfolded before me, but how monotonous, and ill suited to diminish the dejection with which my mind was overwhelmed! For the first time in my life, I found myself under way upon the main sea, with nothing to fix my regards and arrest my attention but the frail machine which bore me between the abyss of waters and the immensity of the skies. I remained for a long time with my eyes fixed in the direction of that land which I no longer saw, and almost despaired of ever seeing again; I made serious reflections on the nature and consequences of the enterprise in which I had so rashly embarked; and I confess that if at that moment the offer had been made to release me from my engagement, I should have accepted the proposal with all my heart. It is true that the hopeless confusion and incumberment of the vessel's deck, the great number of strangers among whom I found myself, the brutal style which the captain and his subalterns used toward our young Canadians; all, in a word, conspired to make me augur a vexatious and disagreeable voyage. The sequel will show that I did not deceive myself in that.

We perceived very soon in the S. W., which was our weather side, a vessel that bore directly toward us; she made a signal that was understood by our captain; we hove to, and stood on her bow. It turned out to be the American frigate *Constitution.* We sent our boat on board of her, and sailed in company till toward five o'clock, when, our papers having been sent back to us, we separated.

The wind having increased, the motion of the vessel made us sea-sick, those of us, I mean, who were for the first time at sea. The weather was fine, however; the vessel, which at first sailing was lumbered in such a manner that we could hardly get in or out of our berths, and scarcely work ship, by little and little got into order, so that we soon found ourselves more at ease.

On the 14th we commenced to take flying fish. The 24th, we saw a great quantity of dolphins. We prepared lines and took two of the latter, which we cooked. The flesh of this fish appeared to me excellent.

After leaving New York, till the 4th of October, we headed southeast. On that day we struck the trade winds, and bore S. S. E.; being, according to our observations, in latitude 17° 43″ and longitude 22° 39″.

On the 5th, in the morning, we came in sight of the Cape-Verd islands, bearing W. N. W., and distant about eight or nine miles, having the coast of Africa to the E. S. E. We should have been very glad to touch at these islands to take in water; but as our vessel was an American bottom, and had on board a number of British subjects, our captain did not think fit to expose himself to meet the English ships-of-war cruising on these coasts, who certainly would not have failed to make a strict search, and to take from us the best part of our crew; which would infallibly have proved disastrous to the object for which we had shipped them.

Speaking of water, I may mention that the rule was to serve it out in rations of a quart a day; but that we were now reduced to a pint and a half. For the rest, our farė consisted of fourteen ounces of hard bread, a pound and a quarter of salt beef or one of pork, per day, and half a pint of souchong tea, with sugar, per man. The pork and beef were served alternately: rice and beans, each once a week; corn-meal pudding with molasses, ditto; on Sundays the steerage passengers were allowed a bottle of Teneriffe wine. All except the four partners, Mr. Lewis, acting as captain's clerk, and Mr. T. M'Kay, were in the steerage; the cabin containing but six berths, besides the captain's and first-mate's state-rooms.

As long as we were near the coast of Africa, we had light and variable winds, and extremely hot weather; on the 8th, we had a dead calm, and saw several sharks round the vessel; we took one which we ate. I found the taste to resemble sturgeon. We experienced on that day an excessive heat, the mercury being at 94° of Fahrenheit. From the 8th to the 11th we had on board a canary bird, which we treated with the greatest care and kindness, but which nevertheless quitted us, probably for a certain death.

The nearer we approached to the equator the more we perceived the heat to increase: on the 16th, in latitude 6°, longitude 22° west from Greenwich, the mercury stood at 108°. We discovered on that day a sail bearing down upon us. The next morning she reappeared, and approached within gun-shot. She was a large brig, carrying about twenty guns: we sailed in company all day by a good breeze, all sail spread; but toward evening she dropped astern and altered her course to the S. S. E.

On the 18th, at daybreak, the watch alarmed us by announcing that the same brig which had followed us the day before, was under our lee, a cable's length off, and seemed desirous of knowing who we were, without showing her own colors. Our captain appeared to be in some alarm; and admitting that she was a better sailer than we, he called all the passengers and crew on deck, the drum beat to quarters, and we feigned to make preparations for combat.

It is well to observe that our vessel mounted ten pieces of cannon, and was pierced for twenty; the forward port-holes were adorned with sham guns. Whether it was our formidable appearance or no, at about ten A. M. the stranger again changed her course, and we soon lost sight of her entirely.

Nothing further remarkable occurred to us till the 22d, when we passed the line in longitude 25° 9′′. According to an ancient custom the crew baptized those of their number who had never before crossed the equator; it was a holyday for them on board. About two o'clock in the afternoon we perceived a sail in the S. S. W. We were not a little alarmed, believing that it was the same brig which we had seen some days before; for it was lying to, as if awaiting our approach. We soon drew near, and to our great joy discovered that she was a Portuguese; we hailed her, and learned that she came from some part of South America, and was bound to Pernambuco, on the coasts of Brazil. Very soon after we began to see what navigators call the *Clouds of Magellan:* they are three little white spots that one perceives in the sky almost as soon as one passes the equator: they were situated in the S. S. W.

The 1st November, we began to see great numbers of aquatic birds. Toward three o'clock P. M., we discovered a sail on our larboard, but did not approach sufficiently near to speak her. The 3d, we saw two more sails, making to the S. E. We passed the tropic of Capricorn on the 4th, with a fine breeze, and in longitude 33° 27″.

We lost the trade-winds, and as we advanced south the weather became cold and rainy. The 11th, we had a calm, although the swell was heavy. We saw several turtles, and the captain having sent out the small boat, we captured two of them. During the night of the 11th and 12th, the wind changed to the N. E., and raised a terrible tempest, in which the gale, the rain, the lightning, and thunder, seemed to have sworn our destruction; the sea appeared all a-fire, while our little vessel was the sport of winds and waves. We kept the hatches closed, which did not prevent us from passing very uncomfortable nights while the storm lasted; for the great heats that we had experienced between the tropics, had so opened the seams of the deck that every time the waves passed over, the water rushed down in quantities upon our hammocks. The 14th, the wind shifted to the S. S. W., which compelled us to beat to windward. During the night we were struck by a tremendous sea; the helm was seized beyond control, and the man at the wheel was thrown from one side of the ship to the other, breaking two of his ribs, which confined him to his berth for a week.

In latitude 35° 19″, longitude 40°, the sea appeared to be covered with marine plants, and the change that we observed in the color of the water, as well as the immense number of gulls and other aquatic birds that we saw, proved to us that we were not far from the mouth of the *Rio de la Plata*. The wind continued to blow furiously till the 21st, when it subsided a little, and the weather cleared up. On the 25th, being in the 46th degree, and 30 minutes of latitude, we saw a penguin.

We began to feel sensibly the want of water: since passing the tropic of Capricorn the daily allowance had been always diminishing, till we were reduced to three gills a day, a slender modicum considering that we had only salt provisions. We had indeed a still, which we used to render the sea-water drinkable; but we distilled merely what sufficed for the daily use of the kitchen, as to do more would have required a great quantity of wood or coal. As we were not more than one hundred and fifty leagues from the Falkland isles, we determined to put in there and endeavor to replenish our casks, and the captain caused the anchors to be got ready.

We had contrary winds from the 27th of November to the 3d December. On the evening of that day, we heard one of the officers, who was at the mast head, cry "Land! Land!" Nevertheless, the night coming on, and the barren rocks which we had before us being little elevated above the ocean, we hove to.

CHAPTER III.

Arrival at the Falkland Isles.—Landing.—Perilous Situation of the Author and some of his Companions.—Portrait of Captain Thorn.—Cape Horn.—Navigation to the Sandwich Islands.

On the 4th (Dec.) in the morning, I was not the last to mount on deck, to feast my eyes with the sight of land; for it is only those who have been three or four months at sea, who know how to appreciate the pleasure which one then feels even at sight of such barren and bristling rocks as form the Falkland Isles. We drew near these rocks very soon, and entered between two of the islands, where we anchored on a good ground. The first mate being sent ashore to look for water, several of our gentlemen accompanied him. They returned in the evening with the disappointing intelligence that they had not been able to find fresh water. They brought us, to compensate for this, a number of wild geese and two seals.

The weather appearing to threaten, we weighed anchor and put out to sea. The night was tempestuous, and in the morning of the 5th we had lost sight of the first islands. The wind blowing off land, it was necessary to beat up all that day; in the evening we found ourselves sufficiently near the shore, and hove to for the night. The 6th brought us a clear sky, and with a fresh breeze we succeeded in gaining a good anchorage, which we took to be Port Egmont, and where we found good water.

On the 7th, we sent ashore the water casks, as well as the cooper to superintend filling them, and the blacksmiths who were occupied in some repairs required by the ship. For our part, having erected a tent near the springs, we passed the time while they were taking in water, in coursing over the isles: we had a boat for our accommodation, and killed every day a great many wild geese and ducks. These birds differ in plumage from those which are seen in Canada.

We also killed a great many seals. These animals ordinarily keep upon the rocks. We also saw several foxes of the species called *Virginia* fox: they were shy and yet fierce, barking like dogs and then flying precipitately. Penguins are also numerous on the Falkland Isles. These birds have a fine plumage, and resemble the loon: but they do not fly, having only little stumps of wings which they use to help themselves in waddling along. The rocks were covered with them. It being their sitting season we found them on their nests, from which they would not stir. They are not wild or timid: far from flying at our approach, they attacked us with their bill, which is very sharp, and with their short wings. The flesh of the penguin is black and leathery, with a strong fishy taste, and one must be very hungry to make up one's mind to eat it. We got a great quantity of eggs by dislodging them from their nests.

As the French and English had both attempted to form establishments on these rocks, we endeavored to find some vestige of them; the tracks which we met everywhere made us hope to find goats also: but all our researches were vain: all that we discovered was an old fishing cabin, constructed of whale bone, and some seal-skin moccasins; for these rocks offer not a single tree to the view, and are frequented solely by the vessels which pursue the whale fishery in the southern seas. We found, however, two head-boards with inscriptions in English, marking the spot where two men had been interred: as the letters were nearly obliterated, we carved new ones on fresh pieces of board procured from the ship. This pious attention to two dead men nearly proved fatal to a greater number of the living; for all the casks having been filled and sent on board, the captain gave orders to re-embark, and without troubling himself to inquire if this order had been executed or not, caused the anchor to be weighed on the morning of the 11th, while I and some of my companions were engaged in erecting the inscriptions of which I have spoken, others were cutting grass for the hogs, and Messrs M'Dougall and D. Stuart had gone to the south side of the isle to look for game.

The roaring of the sea against the rock-bound shore prevented them from hearing the gun, and they did not rejoin us till the vessel was already at sea. We then lost no time, but pushed off, being eight in number, with our little boat, only twenty feet keel. We rowed with all our might, but gained nothing upon the vessel. We were losing sight of the islands at last, and our case seemed desperate. While we paused, and were debating what course to pursue, as we had no compass, we observed the ship tacking and standing toward us. In fine after rowing for three hours and a half, in an excited state of feeling not easily described, we succeeded in regaining the vessel, and were taken on board at about three o'clock P. M.

Having related this trait of malice on the part of our captain, I shall be permitted to make some remarks on his character. Jonathan Thorn was brought up in the naval service of his country, and had distinguished himself in a battle fought between the Americans and the Turks at Tripoli, some years before: he held the rank of first lieutenant. He was a strict disciplinarian, of a quick and passionate temper, accustomed to exact obedience, considering nothing but duty, and giving himself no trouble about the murmurs of his crew, taking counsel of nobody, and following Mr. Astor's instructions to the letter. Such was the man who had been selected to command our ship. His haughty mànners, his rough and overbearing disposition, had lost him the affection of most of the crew and of all the passengers: he knew it, and in consequence sought every opportunity to mortify us. It is true that the passengers had some reason to reproach themselves; they were not free from blame; but he had been the aggressor; and nothing could excuse the act of cruelty and barbarity of which he was guilty, in intending to leave us upon those barren rocks of the Falkland isles, where we must inevitably have perished. This lot was reserved for us, but for the bold interference of Mr. R. Stuart, whose uncle was of our party, and who, seeing that the captain, far from waiting for us, coolly continued his course, threatened to

ENTRANCE OF THE COLUMBIA RIVER.
Ship Tonquin crossing the bar, March 25th, 1811.

blow his brains out unless he hove to and took us on board.

We pursued our course, bearing S. S. W., and on the 14th, in latitude 54° 1′, longitude 64° 13′, we found bottom at sixty-five fathoms, and saw a sail to the south. On the 15th, in the morning, we discovered before us the high mountains of *Terra del fuego*, which we continued to see till evening: the weather then thickened, and we lost sight of them. We encountered a furious storm which drove us to the 56th degree and 18′ of latitude. On the 18th, we were only fifteen leagues from Cape Horn. A dead calm followed, but the current carried us within sight of the cape, five or six leagues distant. This cape, which forms the southern extremity of the American continent, has always been an object of terror to the navigators who have to pass from one sea to the other; several of whom to avoid doubling it, have exposed themselves to the long and dangerous passage of the straits of Magellan, especially when about entering the Pacific ocean. When we saw ourselves under the stupendous rocks of the cape, we felt no other desire but to get away from them as soon as possible, so little agreeable were those rocks to the view, even in the case of people who had been some months at sea! And by the help of a land breeze we succeeded in gaining an offing. While becalmed here, we measured the velocity of the current setting east, which we found to be about three miles an hour.

The wind soon changed again to the S. S. W., and blew a gale. We had to beat. We passed in sight of the islands of Diego Ramirez, and saw a large schooner under their lee. The distance that we had run from New York, was about 9,165 miles. We had frightful weather till the 24th, when we found ourselves in 58° 16′ of south latitude. Although it was the height of summer in that hemisphere, and the days as long as they are at Quebec on the 21st of June (we could read on deck at midnight without artificial light), the cold was nevertheless very great and the air very humid: the mercury for several days was but fourteen degrees above freezing point, by Fahrenheit's thermometer. If such is the temperature in these latitudes at the end of December, corresponding to our June, what must it be in the shortest days of the year, and where can the Patagonians then take refuge, and the inhabitants of the islands so improperly named the Land of Fire!

The wind, which till the 24th had been con trary, hauled round to the south, and we ran westward. The next day being Christmas, we had the satisfaction to learn by our noon-day observation that we had weathered the cape, and were, consequently, now in the Pacific ocean. Up to that date we had but one man attacked with scurvy, a malady to which those who make long voyages are subject, and which is occasioned by the constant use of salt provisions, by the humidity of the vessel, and the inaction.

From the 25th of December till the 1st of January, we were favored with a fair wind and ran eighteen degrees to the north in that short space of time. Though cold yet, the weather was nevertheless very agreeable. On the 17th, in latitude 10° S., and longitude 110° 50′ W., we took several *bonitas*, an excellent fish. We passed the equator on the 23d, in 128° 14′ of west longitude. A great many porpoises came round the vessel. On the 25th arose a tempest which lasted till the 28th. The wind then shifted to the E. S. E. and carried us two hundred and twenty-four miles on our course in twenty-four hours. Then we had several days of contrary winds; on the 8th of February it hauled to the S. E., and on the 11th we saw the peak of a mountain covered with snow, which the first mate, who was familiar with these seas, told me was the summit of *Mona-Roah*, a high mountain on the island of *Ohehy*, one of those which the circumnavigator Cook named the Sandwich Isles, and where he met his death in 1779. We headed to the land all day, and although we made eight or nine knots an hour, it was not till evening that we were near enough to distinguish the huts of the islanders: which is sufficient to prove the prodigious elevation of *Mona Roah* above the level of the sea.

CHAPTER IV.

Accident.—View of the Coast.—Attempted Visit of the Natives. —Their Industry.—Bay of Karaka-koua.—Landing on the Island.—John Young, Governor of Owahee.

We were ranging along the coast with the aid of a fine breeze, when the boy Perrault, who had mounted the fore-rigging to enjoy the scenery, lost his hold, and being to windward where the shrouds were taut, rebounded from them like a ball some twenty feet from the ship's side into the ocean. We perceived his fall and threw over to him chairs, barrels, benches, hen-coops, in a word everything we could lay hands on; then the captain gave the orders to heave to; in the twinkling of an eye the lashings of one of the quarter-boats were cut apart, the boat lowered and manned: by this time the boy was considerably a-stern. He would have been lost undoubtedly but for a wide pair of canvass overalls full of tar and grease, which operated like a life-preserver. His head, however, was under when he was picked up, and he was brought on board lifeless, about a quarter of an hour after he fell into the sea. We succeeded, notwithstanding, in a short time, in bringing him to, and in a few hours he was able to run upon the deck.

The coast of the island, viewed from the sea, offers the most picturesque *coup d'œil*, and the loveliest prospect; from the beach to the mountains the land rises amphitheatrically, all along which is a border of lower country covered with cocoa-trees and bananas, through the thick foliage whereof you perceive the huts of the islanders; the valleys which divide the hills that lie beyond appear well cultivated, and the mountains themselves, though extremely high, are covered with wood to their summits, except those few peaks which glitter with perpetual snow.

As we ran along the coast, some canoes left the beach and came alongside, with vegetables and cocoa-nuts; but as we wished to profit by the breeze to gain the anchorage, we did not think fit to stop. We coasted along during a part of the night; but a calm came on which lasted till the morrow. As we were opposite the bay of Karaka-koua, the natives came out again, in greater numbers, bringing us cabbages, yams, *taro*, bananas, bread-fruit, water-melons, poultry, &c., for which we traded in the way of exchange. Toward evening, by the aid of a sea breeze that rose as day declined, we got inside the harbor where we anchored on a coral bottom in fourteen fathoms water.

The next day the islanders visited the vessel in great numbers all day long, bringing, as on the day before, fruits, vegetables, and some pigs, in exchange for which we gave them glass beads, iron rings, needles, cotton cloth, &c.

Some of our gentlemen went ashore and were astonished to find a native occupied in building a small sloop of about thirty tons: the tools of which he made use consisted of a half worn-out axe, an adze, about two-inch blade, made out of a paring chisel, a saw, and an iron rod which he heated red hot and made it serve the purpose of an auger. It required no little patience and dexterity to achieve anything with such instruments: he was apparently not deficient in these qualities, for his work was tolerably well advanced. Our people took him on board with them, and we supplied him with suitable tools, for which he appeared extremely grateful.

On the 14th, in the morning, while the ship's carpenter was engaged in replacing one of the cat-heads, two composition sheaves fell into the sea; as we had no others on board, the captain proposed to the islanders, who are excellent swimmers, to dive for them, promising a reward; and immediately two offered themselves. They plunged several times, and each time brought up shells as a proof that they had been to the bottom. We had the curiosity to hold our watches while they dove, and were astonished to find that they remained four minutes under the water. That exertion appeared to me, however, to fatigue them a great deal, to such a degree that the blood streamed from their nostrils and ears.

At last one of them brought up the sheaves and received the promised recompense, which consisted of four yards of cotton.

Karaka-koua bay where we lay, may be three quarters of a mile deep, and a mile and a half wide at the entrance: the latter is formed by two low points of rock which appear to have run down from the mountains in the form of lava, after a volcanic eruption. On each point is situated a village of moderate size; that is to say, a small group of the low huts of the islanders. The bottom of the bay terminates in a bold *escarpment* of rock, some four hundred feet high, on the top of which is seen a solitary cocoa-tree.

On the evening of the 14th, I went ashore with some other passengers, and we landed at the group of cabins on the western point, of those which I have described. The inhabitants entertained us with a dance executed by nineteen young women and one man, all singing together, and in pretty good time. An old man showed us the spot where Captain Cook was killed, on the 14th of February, 1779, with the cocoa-nut trees pierced by the balls from the boats which the unfortunate navigator commanded. This old man, whether it were feigned or real sensibility, seemed extremely affected and even shed tears, in showing us these objects. As for me, I could not help finding it a little singular to be thus, by mere chance, upon this spot, on the 14th of February, 1811; that is to say, thirty-two years after, on the anniversary of the catastrophe which has rendered it for ever celebrated. I drew no sinister augury from the coincidence, however, and returned to the ship with my companions as gay as I left it. When I say with my companions, I ought to except the boatswain, John Anderson, who, having had several altercations with the captain on the passage, now deserted the ship, preferring to live with the natives rather than obey any longer so uncourteous a superior. A sailor also deserted; but the islanders brought him back, at the request of the captain. They offered to bring back Anderson, but the captain preferred leaving him behind.

We found no good water near Karaka-koua bay: what the natives brought us in gourds was brackish. We were also in great want of fresh meat, but could not obtain it: the king of these islands having expressly forbidden his subjects to supply any to the vessels which touched there. One of the chiefs sent a canoe to Tohehigh bay, to get from the governor of the island, who resided there, permission to sell us some pigs. The messengers returned the next day, and brought us a letter, in which the governor ordered us to proceed without delay to the isle of Wahoo, where the king lives; assuring us that we should there find good water and everything else we needed.

We got under way on the 16th, and with a light wind coasted the island as far as Tohehigh bay. The wind then dropping away entirely, the captain, accompanied by Messrs. M'Kay and M'Dougall, went ashore, to pay a visit to the governor aforesaid. He was not a native, but a Scotchman named John Young, who came hither some years after the death of Captain Cook.

This man had married a native woman, and had so gained the friendship and confidence of the king, as to be raised to the rank of chief and after the conquest of Wahoo by King Tamehameha, was made governor of Owhyhee (Hawaii) the most considerable of the Sandwich Islands, both by its extent and population. His excellency explained to our gentlemen the reason why the king had interdicted the trade in hogs to the inhabitants of all the islands: this reason being that his majesty wished to reserve to himself the monopoly of that branch of commerce, for the augmentation of his royal revenue by its exclusive profits. The governor also informed them that no rain had fallen on the south part of Hawaii for three years; which explained why we found so little fresh water: he added that the north part of the island was more fertile than the south, where we were: but that there was no good anchorage: that part of the coast being defended by sunken rocks which form heavy breakers. In fine, the governor dismissed our gentlemen with a present of four fine fat hogs; and we, in return, sent him some tea, coffee, and chocolate, and a keg of Madeira wine.

The night was nearly a perfect calm, and on the 17th we found ourselves abreast of *Mona-Wororayea* a snow-capped mountain, like *Mona-Roah*, but which appeared to me less lofty than the latter. A number of islanders came to visit us as before, with some objects of curiosity, and some small fresh fish. The wind rising on the 18th, we soon passed the western extremity of Hawaii, and sailed by Mowhee and Tahooraha, two more islands of this group, and said to be, like the rest, thickly inhabited. The first presents a highly picturesque aspect, being composed of hills rising in the shape of a sugar loaf and completely covered with cocoa-nut and bread-fruit trees.

At last, on the 21st, we approached Wahoo, and came to anchor opposite the bay of *Ohetity*, outside the bar, at a distance of some two miles from the land.

CHAPTER V.

Bay of Ohetity.—Tamehameha, King of the Islands.—His Visit to the Ship.—His Capital.—His Naval Force.—His Authority.—Productions of the Country.—Manners and Customs.—Reflections.

THERE is no good anchorage in the bay of Ohetity, inside the bar or coral reef: the holding-ground is bad: so that, in case of a storm, the safety of the ship would have been endangered. Moreover, with a contrary wind, it would have been difficult to get out of the inner harbor; for which reasons, our captain preferred to remain in the road. For the rest, the country surrounding the bay is even more lovely in aspect than that of Karaka-koua; the mountains rise to a less elevation in the back-ground, and the soil has an appearance of greater fertility.

Tamehameha, whom all the Sandwich Isles

obeyed when we were there in 1811, was neither the son nor the relative of Tierroboo, who reigned in Owhyhee (Hawaii) in 1779, when Captain Cook and some of his people were massacred. He was, at that date, but a chief of moderate power; but, being skilful, intriguing, and full of ambition, he succeeded in gaining a numerous party, and finally possessed himself of the sovereignty. As soon as he saw himself master of Owhyhee, his native island, he meditated the conquest of the leeward islands, and in a few years he accomplished it. He even passed into *Atouay*, the most remote of all, and vanquished the ruler of it, but contented himself with imposing on him an annual tribute. He had fixed his residence at Wahoo, because of all the Sandwich Isles it was the most fertile, the most picturesque—in a word, the most worthy of the residence of the sovereign.

As soon as we arrived, we were visited by a canoe manned by three white men, Davis and Wadsworth, Americans, and Manini, a Spaniard. The last offered to be our interpreter during our stay; which was agreed to. Tamehameha presently sent to us his prime-minister, *Kraimoku*, to whom the Americans have given the name of *Pitt*, on account of his skill in the affairs of government. Our captain, accompanied by some of our gentlemen, went ashore immediately, to be presented to Tamehameha. About four o'clock, P. M., we saw them returning, accompanied by a double pirogue conveying the king and his suite. We ran up our colors, and received his majesty with a salute of four guns.

Tamehameha was above the middle height, well made, robust and inclined to corpulency, and had a majestic carriage. He appeared to me from fifty to sixty years old. He was clothed in the European style, and wore a sword. He walked a long time on the deck, asking explanations in regard to those things which he had not seen on other vessels, and which were found on ours. A thing which appeared to surprise him, was to see that we could render the water of the sea fresh, by means of the still attached to our caboose; he could not imagine how that could be done. We invited him into the cabin, and, having regaled him with some glasses of wine, began to talk of business matters: we offered him merchandise in exchange for hogs, but were not able to conclude the bargain that day. His majesty re-embarked in his double pirogue, at about six o'clock in the evening. It was manned by twenty-four men. A great chest, containing firearms, was lashed over the centre of the two canoes forming the pirogue; and it was there that Tamehameha sat, with his prime-minister at his side.

In the morning, on the 22d, we sent our water-casks ashore and filled them with excellent water. At about noon his sable majesty paid us another visit, accompanied by his three wives and his favorite minister. These females were of an extraordinary corpulence, and of unmeasured size. They were dressed in the fashion of the country, having nothing but a piece of *tapa*, or bark-cloth, about two yards long, passed round the hips and falling to the knees. We resumed the negotiations of the day before, and were more successful. I remarked that when the bargain was concluded, he insisted with great pertinacity that part of the payment should be in Spanish dollars. We asked the reason, and he made answer that he wished to buy a frigate of his brother, King George, meaning the king of England. The bargain concluded, we prayed his majesty and his suite to dine with us; they consented, and toward evening retired, apparently well satisfied with their visit and our reception of them.

In the meantime, the natives surrounded the ship in great numbers, with hundreds of canoes, offering us their goods, in the shape of eatables and the rude manufactures of the island, in exchange for merchandise; but, as they had also brought intoxicating liquors in gourds, some of the crew got drunk; the captain was, consequently, obliged to suspend the trade, and forbade any one to traffic with the islanders, except through the first-mate, who was intrusted with that business.

I landed on the 22d, with Messrs. Pillet and

M'Gillis: we passed the night ashore, spending that day and the next morning in rambling over the environs of the bay, followed by a crowd of men, women, and children.

Ohetity, where Tamehameha resides, and which, consequently, may be regarded as the capital of his kingdom, is—or at least was at that time—a moderate-sized city, or rather a large village. Besides the private houses, of which there were perhaps two hundred, constructed of poles planted in the ground and covered over with matting, there were the royal palace, which was not magnificent by any means: a public store, of two stories, one of stone and the other of wood; two *morais*, or idol temples, and a wharf. At the latter we found an old vessel, the *Lady Bird*, which some American navigators had given in exchange for a schooner; it was the only large vessel which King Tamehameha possessed; and, besides, was worth nothing. As for schooners he had forty of them, of from twenty to thirty tons burthen: these vessels served to transport the tributes in kind paid by his vassals in the other islands. Before the Europeans arrived among these savages, the latter had no means of communication between one isle and another, but their canoes, and as some of the islands are not in sight of each other, these voyages must have been dangerous. Near the palace I found an Indian from Bombay, occupied in making a twelve inch cable, for the use of the ship which I have described.

Tamehameha kept constantly round his house a guard of twenty-four men. These soldiers wore, by way of uniform, a long blue coat with yellow; and each was armed with a musket. In front of the house, on an open square, were placed fourteen four-pounders, mounted on their carriages.

The king was absolute, and judged in person the differences between his subjects. We had an opportunity of witnessing a proof of it, the day after our landing. A Portuguese having had a quarrel with a native, who was intoxicated, struck him: immediately the friends of the latter, who had been the aggressor after all, gathered in a crowd to beat down the poor foreigner with stones; he fled as fast as he could to the house of the king, followed by a mob of enraged natives, who nevertheless stopped at some distance from the guards, while the Portuguese, all breathless, crouched in a corner. We were on the esplanade in front of the palace royal, and curiosity to see the trial led us into the presence of his majesty, who having caused the quarrel to be explained to him, and heard the witnesses on both sides, condemned the native to work four days in the garden of the Portuguese and to give him a hog. A young Frenchman from Bordeaux, preceptor of the king's sons, whom he taught to read, and who understood the language, acted as interpreter to the Portuguese, and explained to us the sentence. I can not say whether our presence influenced the decision, or whether, under other circumstances, the Portuguese would have been less favorably treated. We were given to understand that Tamehameha was pleased to see whites establish themselves in his dominions, but that he esteemed only people with some useful trade, and despised idlers, and especially drunkards. We saw at Wahoo about thirty of these white inhabitants, for the most part, people of no character, and who had remained on the islands either from indolence, or from drunkenness and licentiousness. Some had taken wives in the country, in which case the king gave them a portion of land to cultivate for themselves. But two of the worst sort had found means to procure a small still, wherewith they manufactured rum and supplied it to the natives.

The first navigators found only four sorts of quadrupeds on the Sandwich islands:—dogs, swine, lizards, and rats. Since then sheep have been carried there, goats, horned cattle, and even horses, and these animals have multiplied.

The chief vegetable productions of these isles are the sugar cane, the bread-fruit tree, the banana, the water-melon, the musk-melon, the *taro*, the *ava*, the *pandanus*, the mulberry, &c. The bread-fruit tree is about the size of a large apple-tree; the fruit resembles an apple and is about twelve or fourteen inches in circumference; the rind is thick and rough like a melon: when cut transversely it is found to be full of sacs, like the inside of an orange; the pulp has the consistence of water-melon, and is cooked before it is eaten. We saw orchards of bread-fruit trees and bananas, and fields of sugar-cane, back of Ohetity.

The *taro* grows in low situations, and demands a great deal of care. It is not unlike a white turnip,* and as it constitutes the principal food of the natives, it is not to be wondered at that they bestow so much attention on its culture. Wherever a spring of pure water is found issuing out of the side of a hill, the gardener marks out on the declivity the size of the field he intends to plant. The ground is levelled and surrounded with a mud or stone wall, not exceeding eighteen inches in height, and having a flood gate above and below. Into this enclosure the water of the spring is conducted, or is suffered to escape from it, according to the dryness of the season. When the root has acquired a sufficient size it is pulled up for immediate use. This es-

* Bougainville calls it "Calf-foot root."

culent is very bad to eat raw, but boiled it is better than the yam. Cut in slices, dried, pounded and reduced to a farina, it forms with bread fruit the principal food of the natives. Sometimes they boil it to the consistence of porridge, which they put into gourds and allow to ferment; it will then keep a long time. They also use to mix with it; fish, which they commonly eat raw with the addition of a little salt, obtained by evaporation.

The *ava* is a plant more injurious than useful to the inhabitants of these isles; since they only make use of it to obtain a dangerous and intoxicating drink, which they also call *ava*. The mode of preparing this beverage is as follows: they chew the root, and spit out the result into a basin; the juice thus expressed is exposed to the sun to undergo fermentation; after which they decant it into a gourd; it is then fit for use, and they drink it on occasions to intoxication. The too frequent use of this disgusting liquor causes loss of sight, and a sort of leprosy, which can only be cured by abstaining from it, and by bathing frequently in the water of the sea. This leprosy turns their skin white: we saw several of the lepers, who were also blind, or nearly so. The natives are also fond of smoking: the tobacco grows in the islands, but I believe it has been introduced from abroad. The bark of the mulberry furnishes the cloth worn by both sexes; of the leaves of the *pandanus* they make mats. They have also a kind of wax-nut, about the size of a dried plum of which they make candles by running a stick through several of them. Lighted at one end, they burn like a wax taper, and are the only light they use in their huts at night.

The men are generally well made and tall: they wear for their entire clothing what they call a *maro;* it is a piece of figured or white tapa, two yards long and a foot wide, which they pass round the loins and between the legs, tying the ends in a knot over the left hip. At first sight I thought they were painted red, but soon perceived that it was the natural color of their skin. The women wear a petticoat of the same stuff as the *maro*, but wider and longer, without, however, reaching below the knees. They have sufficiently regular features, and but for the color, may pass, generally speaking, for handsome women. Some to heighten their charms, dye their black hair (cut short for the purpose) with quick lime, forming round the head a strip of pure white, which disfigures them monstrously. Others among the young wear a more becoming garland of flowers. For other traits, they are very lascivious, and far from observing a modest reserve, especially toward strangers. In regard to articles of mere ornament, I was told that they were not the same in all the island. I did not see them, either, clothed in their war dresses, or habits of ceremony. But I had an opportunity to see them paint or print their *tapa*, or bark cloth, an occupation in which they employ a great deal of care and patience. The pigments they use are derived from vegetable juices, prepared with the oil of the cocoa-nut. Their pencils are little reeds or canes of bamboo, at the extremity of which they carve out divers sorts of flowers. First they tinge the cloth they mean to print, yellow, green, or some other color which forms the ground: then they draw upon it perfectly straight lines, without any other guide but the eye; lastly they dip the ends of the bamboo sticks in paint of a different tint from the ground, and apply them between the dark or bright bars thus formed. This cloth resembles a good deal our calicoes and printed cottons; the oils with which it is impregnated renders it impervious to water. It is said that the natives of *Atowy* excel all the other islanders in the art of painting the tapa.

The Sandwich-islanders live in villages of one or two hundred houses arranged without symmetry, or rather grouped together in complete defiance of it. These houses are constructed (as I have before said) of posts driven in the ground, covered with long dry grass, and walled with matting; the thatched roof gives them a sort of resemblance to our Canadian barns or granges. The length of each house varies according to the number of the family which occupies it: they are not smoky like the wigwams of our Indians, the fireplace being always outside in the open air, where all the cooking is performed. Hence their dwellings are very clean and neat inside.

Their pirogues or canoes are extremely light and neat: those which are single have an outrigger, consisting of two curved pieces of timber lashed across the bows, and touching the water at the distance of five or six feet from the side; another piece, turned up at each extremity, is tied to the end and drags in the water, on which it acts like a skating iron on the ice, and by its weight keeps the canoe in equilibrium: without that contrivance they would infallibly upset. Their paddles are long, with a very broad blade. All these canoes carry a lateen, or sprit-sail, which is made of a mat of grass or leaves, extremely well woven.

I did not remain long enough with these people to acquire very extensive and exact notions of their religion: I know that they recognise a Supreme Being, whom they call *Etoway*, and a number of inferior divinities. Each village has one or more *morais*. These morais are enclosures which served for cemeteries; in the middle is a temple, where the priests alone have a right to enter: they contain several idols of wood, rudely sculptured. At the feet of these images are deposited, and left to putrify, the offerings of the people, consisting of dogs, pigs, fowls, vegetables, &c. The respect of these savages for their priests extends almost to adoration; they regard their persons as sacred, and feel the greatest scruple in touching the objects, or going near the places, which they have declared *taboo* or forbidden. The *taboo* has often been useful to European navigators, by freeing them from the importunities of the crowd.

In our rambles we met groups playing at different games. That of draughts appeared the most common. The checker-board is very simple, the squares being marked on the ground with a sharp stick: the men are merely shells or pebbles. The game was different from that played in civilized countries, so that we could not understand it.

Although nature has done almost everything

for the inhabitants of the Sandwich islands—though they enjoy a perpetual spring, a clear sky, a salubrious climate, and scarcely any labor is required to produce the necessaries of life—they can not be regarded as generally happy: the artisans and producers, whom they call *Tootoos*, are nearly in the same situation as the Helots among the Lacedemonians, condemned to labor almost incessantly for their lord or *Eris*, without hope of bettering their condition, and even restricted in the choice of their daily food.* How has it happened that among a people yet barbarous, where knowledge is nearly equally distributed, the class which is beyond comparison the most numerous has voluntarily submitted to such a humiliating and oppressive yoke? The Tartars, though infinitely less numerous than the Chinese, have subjected them, because the former were warlike and the latter were not. The same thing has happened, no doubt, at remote

* The *Tootoos* and all the women, the wives of the king and principal chiefs excepted, are eternally condemned to the use of fruits and vegetables; dogs and pigs being exclusively reserved for the table of the *Eris*.

periods, in Poland, and other regions of Europe and Asia. If moral causes are joined to physical ones, the superiority of one caste and the inferiority of the other will be still more marked; it is known that the natives of Hispaniola, when they saw the Spaniards arrive on their coast, in vessels of an astonishing size to their apprehensions, and heard them imitate the thunder with their cannon, took them for beings of a superior nature to their own. Supposing that this island had been extremely remote from every other country, and that the Spaniards, after conquering it, had held no further communication with any civilized land, at the end of a century or two the language and the manners would have assimilated, but there would have been two castes, one of lords, enjoying all the advantages, the other of serfs, charged with all the burdens. This theory seems to have been realized anciently in Hindostan; but if we must credit the tradition of the Sandwich-islanders, their country was originally peopled by a man and woman, who came to Owyhee in a canoe. Unless, then, they mean that this man and woman came with their slaves, and that the *Eris* are descended from the first, and the *Tootoos* from the last, they ought to attribute to each other the same origin, and consequently regard each other as equals, and even as brothers, according to the manner of thinking that prevails among savages. The cause of the slavery of women among most barbarous tribes, is more easily explained: the men have subjected them by the right of the strongest, if ignorance and superstition have not caused them to be previously regarded as beings of an inferior nature, made to be servants and not companions.*

* Some Indian tribes think that women have no souls. but die altogether like the brutes; others assign them a different paradise from that of men, which indeed they might have reason to prefer for themselves, unless their relative condition were to be ameliorated in the next world.

CHAPTER VI.

Departure from Wahoo.—Storm.—Arrival at the Mouth of the Columbia.—Reckless Order of the Captain.—Difficulty of the Entrance.—Perilous Situation of the Ship.—Unhappy Fate of a part of the Crew and People of the Expedition.

HAVING taken on board a hundred head of live hogs, some goats, two sheep, a quantity of poultry, two boat-loads of sugar-cane, to feed the hogs, as many more of yams, taro, and other vegetables, and all our water-casks being snugly stowed, we weighed anchor on the 28th of February, sixteen days after our arrival at Karakakoua.

We left another man (Edward Aymes) at Wahoo. He belonged to a boat's crew which was sent ashore for a load of sugar-canes. By the time the boat was loaded by the natives the ebb of the tide had left her aground, and Aymes asked leave of the coxswain to take a stroll, engaging to be back for the flood. Leave was granted him, but during his absence, the tide having come in sufficiently to float the boat, James Thorn, the coxswain, did not wait for the young sailor, who was thus left behind. The captain immediately missed the man, and, on being informed that he had strolled away from the boat on leave, flew into a violent passion. Aymes soon made his appearance alongside, having hired some natives to take him on board; on perceiving him, the captain ordered him to stay in the long-boat, then lashed to the side with its load of sugar-cane. The captain then himself got into the boat, and, taking one of the canes, beat the poor fellow most unmercifully with it; after which, not satisfied with this act of brutality, he seized his victim and threw him overboard! Aymes, however, being an excellent swimmer, made for the nearest native canoe, of which there were, as usual, a great number around the ship. The islanders, more humane than our captain, took in the poor fellow, who, in spite of his entreaties to be received on board, could only succeed in getting his clothes, which were thrown into the canoe. At parting, he told Captain Thorn that he knew enough of the laws of his country, to obtain redress, should they ever meet in the territory of the American Union.

While we were getting under sail, Mr. M'Kay pointed out to the captain that there was one water-cask empty, and proposed sending it ashore to be filled, as the great number of live animals we had on board required a large quantity of fresh water. The captain, who feared that some of the men would desert if he sent them ashore, made an observation to that effect in answer to Mr. M'Kay, who then proposed sending me on a canoe which lay alongside, to fill the cask in question: this was agreed to by the captain, and I took the cask accordingly to the nearest spring. Having filled it, not without some difficulty, the islanders seeking to detain me, and I perceiving that they had given me some gourds full of salt water, I was forced also to demand a double pirogue (for the canoe which had brought the empty cask, was found inadequate to carry a full one), the ship being already under full sail and gaining an offing. As the natives would not lend a hand to procure what I wanted, I thought it necessary to have recourse to the king, and in fact did so. For seeing the vessel so far at sea, with what I knew of the captain's disposition, I began to fear that he had formed the plan of leaving me on the island. My fears, nevertheless were ill-founded; the vessel made a tack toward the shore, to my great joy; and a double pirogue was furnished me, through the good offices of our young friend the French schoolmaster, to return on board with my cask.

Our deck was now as much encumbered as when we left New York; for we had been obliged to place our live animals at the gangways, and to board over their pens, on which it was necessary to pass, to work ship. Our own numbers were also augmented; for we had taken a dozen islanders for the service of our intended commercial establishment. Their term of engagement was three years, during which we were to feed and clothe them, and at its expiration they were to receive a hundred dollars in merchandise. The captain had shipped another dozen as hands on the coasting voyage. These people, who make very good sailors, were eager to be taken into employment, and we might easily have carried off a much greater number.

We had contrary winds till the 2d of March, when, having doubled the western extremity of the island, we made northing, and lost sight of these smiling and temperate countries, to enter very soon a colder region and less worthy of being inhabited. The winds were variable, and nothing extraordinary happened to us till the 16th, when, being arrived at the latitude of 35° 11′ north, and in 138° 16′ of west longitude, the wind shifted all of a sudden to the S. S. W., and blew with such violence, that we were forced to strike top-gallant masts and top-sails, and run before the gale with a double reef in our foresail. The rolling of the vessel was greater than in all the gales we had experienced previously. Nevertheless, as we made great headway, and were approaching the continent, the captain by way of precaution, lay to for two nights successively. At last, on the 22d, in the morning, we saw the land. Although we had not been able to take any observations for several days, nevertheless, by the appearance of the coast, we perceived that we were near the mouth of the river Columbia, and were not more than three miles from land. The breakers formed by the bar at the entrance of that river, and which we could distinguish from the ship, left us no room to doubt that we had arrived at last at the end of our voyage.

The wind was blowing in heavy squalls, and the sea ran very high: in spite of that, the captain caused a boat to be lowered, and Mr. Fox (first mate), Basile Lapensee, Ignace Lapensee, Jos. Nadeau, and John Martin, got into her, taking some provisions and firearms, with orders to sound the channel and report themselves on board as soon as possible. The boat was not even supplied with a good sail, or a mast, but one of the partners gave Mr. Fox a pair of bed sheets to serve for the former. Messrs M'Kay and M'Dougall could not help remonstrating with the captain on the imprudence of sending the boat ashore in such weather; but they could not move his obstinacy. The boat's crew pulled away from the ship; alas! we were never to see her again; and we already had a foreboding of her fate. The next day the wind seemed to moderate, and we approached very near the coast. The entrance of the river, which we plainly distinguished with the naked eye, appeared but a confused and agitated sea: the waves, impelled by a wind from the offing, broke upon the bar, and left no perceptible passage. We got no sign of the boat; and toward evening, for our own safety, we hauled off to sea, with all countenances extremely sad, not excepting the captain's, who appeared to me as much afflicted as the rest, and who had reason to be so. During the night, the wind fell, the clouds dispersed, and the sky became serene. On the morning of the 24th, we found that the current had carried us near the coast again, and we dropped anchor in fourteen fathoms water, north of Cape Disappointment. The *coup d'œil* is not so smiling by a great deal at this anchorage, as at the Sandwich islands, the coast offering little to the eye but a continuous range of high mountains covered with snow.

Although it was calm, the sea continued to break over the reef with violence, between Cape Disappointment and Point Adams. We sent Mr. Mumford (the second mate) to sound a passage; but having found the breakers too heavy, he returned on board about mid-day. Messrs. M'Kay and D. Stuart offered their services to go ashore, to search for the boat's crew who left on the 22d: but they could not find a place to land. They saw Indians, who made signs to them to pull round the cape, but they deemed it more prudent to return to the vessel. Soon after their return, a gentle breeze sprang up from the westward, we raised anchor, and approached the entrance of the river. Mr. Aikin was then despatched in the pinnace, accompanied by John Coles (sailmaker), Stephen Weeks (armorer), and two Sandwich-islanders; and we followed under easy

View of the Falkland Islands.

sail. Another boat had been sent out before this one, but the captain judging that she bore too far south, made her a signal to return. Mr. Aikin not finding less than four fathoms, we followed him and advanced between the breakers, with a favorable wind, so that we passed the boat on our starboard, within pistol-shot. We made signs to her to return on board, but she could not accomplish it; the ebb tide carried her with such rapidity that in a few minutes we had lost sight of her amidst the tremendous breakers that surrounded us. It was near nightfall, the wind began to give way, and the water was so low with the ebb, that we struck six or seven times with violence: the breakers broke over the ship and threatened to submerge her. At last we passed from two and three quarters fathoms of water to seven, where we were obliged to drop anchor, the wind having entirely failed us. We were far, however, from being out of danger, and the darkness came to add to the horror of our situation: our vessel, though at anchor, threatened to be carried away every moment by the tide; the best bower was let go, and it kept two men at the wheel to hold her head in the right direction. However, Providence came to our succor: the flood succeeded to the ebb, and the wind rising out of the offing, we weighed both anchors, in spite of the obscurity of the night, and succeeded in gaining a little bay or cove, formed at the entrance of the river by Cape Disappointment, and called *Baker's Bay*, where we found a good anchorage. It was about midnight, and all retired to take a little rest: the crew, above all, had great need of it. We were fortunate to be in a place of safety, for the wind rose higher and higher during the rest of the night, and on the morning of the 25th allowed us to see that this ocean is not always pacific.

Some natives visited us this day, bringing with them beaver-skins; but the inquietude caused in our minds by the loss of two boats' crews, for whom we wished to make search, did not permit us to think of traffic. We tried to make the savages comprehend, by signs, that we had sent a boat ashore three days previous, and that we had no news of her; but they seemed not to understand us. The captain, accompanied by some of our gentlemen, landed, and they set themselves to search for our missing people, in the woods, and along the shore N. W. of the cape. After a few hours we saw the captain return with Weeks, one of the crew of the last boat sent out. He was stark naked, and after being clothed, and receiving some nourishment, gave us an account of his almost miraculous escape from the waves on the preceding night, in nearly the following terms:—

"After you had passed our boat," said he, "the breakers caused by the meeting of the wind roll and ebb-tide, became a great deal heavier than when we entered the river with the flood. The boat, for want of a rudder, became very hard to manage, and we let her drift at the mercy of the tide, till, after having escaped several surges, one struck us midship and capsized us. I lost sight of Mr. Aiken and John Coles: but the two islanders were close by me; I saw them stripping off their clothes, and I followed their example; and seeing the pinnace within my reach, keel upward, I seized it; the two natives came to my assistance; we righted her, and by sudden jerks threw out so much of the water that she would hold a man: one of the natives jumped in, and, bailing with his two hands, succeeded in a short time in emptying her. The other native found the oars, and about dark we were all three embarked. The tide having now carried us outside the breakers, I endeavored to persuade my companions in misfortune to row, but they were so benumbed with cold that they absolutely refused. I well knew that without clothing, and exposed to the rigor of the air, I must keep in constant exercise. Seeing besides that the night was advancing, and having no resource but the little strength left me, I set to work sculling, and pushed off the bar, but so as not to be carried out too far to sea. About midnight, one of my companions died: the other threw himself upon the body of his comrade, and I could not persuade him to abandon it. Daylight appeared at last; and, being near the shore, I headed in for it, and arrived, thank God, safe and sound, through the breakers, on a sandy beach. I helped the islander, who yet gave some signs of life, to get out of the boat, and we both took to the woods; but, seeing that he was not able to follow me, I left him to his bad fortune, and, pursuing a beaten path that I perceived, I found myself, to my great astonishment, in the course of a few hours, near the vessel."

The gentlemen who went ashore with the captain divided themselves into three parties, to search for the native whom Weeks had left at the entrance of the forest; but, after scouring the woods and the point of the cape all day, they came on board in the evening without having found him.

CHAPTER VII.

Regrets of the Author at the Loss of his Companions.—Obsequies of a Sandwich Islander.—First steps in the Formation of the intended Establishment.—New Alarm.—Encampment.

THE narrative of Weeks informed us of the death of three of our companions, and we could not doubt that the five others had met a similar fate. This loss of eight of our number, in two days, before we had set foot on shore, was a bad augury, and was sensibly felt by all of us. In the course of so long a passage, the habit of seeing each other every day, the participation of the same cares and dangers, and confinement to the same narrow limits, had formed between all the passengers a connection that could not be broken, above all in a manner so sad and so unlooked for, without making us feel a void like that which is experienced in a well-regulated and loving family, when it is suddenly deprived by death, of the presence of one of its cherished members. We had left New York, for the most part strangers to one another; but arrived at the river Columbia we were all friends, and regarded each other almost as brothers. We regretted especially the two brothers Lapensée and Joseph Nadeau: these young men had been in an especial manner recommended by their respectable parents in Canada to the care of Mr. M'Kay; and had acquired by their good conduct the esteem of the captain, of the crew, and of all the passengers. The brothers Lapensée were courageous and willing, never flinching in the hour of danger, and had become as good seamen as any on board. Messrs Fox and Aikin were both highly regarded by all; the loss of Mr. Fox, above all, who was endeared to every one by his gentlemanly behavior and affability, would have been severely regretted at any time, but it was doubly so in the present conjuncture: this gentleman, who had already made a voyage to the

Northwest, could have rendered important services to the captain and to the company. The preceding days had been days of apprehension and of uneasiness; this was one of sorrow and mourning.

The following day, the same gentlemen who had volunteered their services to seek for the missing islander, resumed their labors, and very soon after they left us, we perceived a great fire kindled at the verge of the woods, over against the ship. I was sent in a boat and arrived at the fire. It was our gentlemen who had kindled it, to restore animation to the poor islander, whom they had at last found under the rocks, half dead with cold and fatigue, his legs swollen and his feet bleeding. We clothed him, and brought him on board, where, by our care, we succeeded in restoring him to life.

Toward evening, a number of the Sandwich-islanders, provided with the necessary utensils, and offerings consisting of biscuit, lard, and tobacco, went ashore, to pay the last duties to their compatriot, who died in Mr. Aikin's boat, on the night of the 24th. Mr. Pillet and I went with them, and witnessed the obsequies, which took place in the manner following. Arrived at the spot where the body had been hung upon a tree to preserve it from the wolves, the natives dug a grave in the sand; then taking down the body, and stretching it alongside the pit, they placed the biscuit under one of the arms, a piece of pork beneath the other, and the tobacco beneath the chin and the genital parts. Thus provided for the journey to the other world, the body was deposited in the grave and covered with sand and stones. All the countrymen of the dead man then knelt on either side of the grave, in a double row, with their faces to the east, except one of them who officiated as priest; the latter went to the margin of the sea, and having filled his hat with water, sprinkled the two rows of islanders, and recited a sort of prayer, to which the others responded, nearly as we do in the litanies. That prayer ended, they rose and returned to the vessel, looking neither to the right hand nor to the left. As every one of them appeared to me familiar with the part he performed, it is more than probable that they observed, as far as circumstances permitted, the ceremonies practised in their country on like occasions. We all returned on board about sundown.

The next day, the 27th, desirous of clearing the gangways of the live stock, we sent some men on shore to construct a pen, and soon after landed about fifty hogs, committing them to the care of one of the hands. On the 30th, the long boat was manned, armed and provisioned, and the captain, with Messrs. M'Kay and D. Stuart, and some of the clerks, embarked on it, to ascend the river and choose an eligible spot for our trading establishment. Messrs. Ross and Pillet left at the same time, to run down south, and try to obtain intelligence of Mr. Fox and his crew. In the meantime, having reached some of the goods most at hand, we commenced, with the natives who came every day to the vessel, a trade for beaver-skins, and sea-otter stones.

Messrs. Ross and Pillet returned on board on the 1st of April, without having learned anything respecting Mr. Fox and his party. They did not even perceive along the beach any vestiges of the boat. The natives who occupy Point *Adams*, and who are called *Clatsops*, received our young gentlemen very amicably and hospitably. The captain and his companions also returned on the 4th, without having decided on a position for the establishment, finding none which appeared to them eligible. It was consequently resolved to explore the south bank, and Messrs. M'Dougal and D. Stuart departed on that expedition the next day, promising to return by the 7th.

The 7th came, and these gentlemen did not return. It rained almost all day. The day after, some natives came on board, and reported that Messrs. M'Dougal and Stuart had capsized the evening before in crossing the bay. This news at first alarmed us; and, if it had been verified, would have given the finishing blow to our discouragement. Still, as the weather was excessively bad, and we did not repose entire faith in the story of the natives—whom, moreover, we might not have perfectly understood—

we remained in suspense till the 10th. On the morning of that day, we were preparing to send some of the people in search of our two gentlemen, when we perceived two large canoes, full of Indians, coming toward the vessel: they were of the *Chinook* village, which was situated at the foot of a bluff on the north side of the river, and were bringing back Messrs. M'Dougal and Stuart. We made known to these gentlemen the report we had heard on the 8th from the natives, and they informed us that it had been in fact well founded; that on the 7th, desirous of reaching the ship agreeably to their promise, they had quitted *Chinook* point, in spite of the remonstrances of the chief, *Comcomly*, who sought to detain them by pointing out the danger to which they would expose themselves in crossing the bay in such a heavy sea as it was; that they had scarcely made more than a mile and a half before a huge wave broke over their boat and capsized it; that the Indians, aware of the danger to which they were exposed, had followed them, and that, but for their assistance, Mr. M'Dougal, who could not swim, would inevitably have been drowned; that, after the Chinooks had kindled a large fire and dried their clothes, they had been conducted by them back to their village, where the principal chief had received them with all imaginable hospitality, regaling them with every delicacy his wigwam afforded; that, in fine, if they had got back safe and sound to the vessel, it was to the timely succor and humane cares of the Indians whom we saw before us that they owed it. We liberally rewarded these generous children of the forest, and they returned home well satisfied.

This last survey was also fruitless, as Messrs. M'Dougal and Stuart did not find an advantageous site to build upon. But, as the captain wished to take advantage of the fine season to pursue his traffic with the natives along the N. W. coast, it was resolved to establish ourselves on Point *George*, situated on the south bank, about fourteen or fifteen miles from our present anchorage. Accordingly, we embarked on the 12th, in the long-boat, to the number of twelve, furnished with tools, and with provisions for a week. We landed at the bottom of a small bay, where we formed a sort of encampment. The spring, usually so tardy in this latitude, was already far advanced; the foliage was budding, and the earth was clothing itself with verdure; the weather was superb, and all nature smiled. We imagined ourselves in the garden of Eden; the wild forests seemed to us delightful groves, and the leaves transformed to brilliant flowers. No doubt, the pleasure of finding ourselves at the end of our voyage, and liberated from the ship, made things appear to us a great deal more beautiful than they really were. Be that as it may, we set ourselves to work with enthusiasm, and cleared, in a few days, a point of land of its under-brush, and of the huge trunks of pine-trees that covered it, which we rolled, half-burnt, down the bank. The vessel came to moor near our encampment, and the trade went on. The natives visited us constantly and in great numbers; some to trade, others to gratify their curiosity, or to purloin some little articles if they found an opportunity. We landed the frame timbers which we had brought, ready cut for the purpose, in the vessel; and by the end of April, with the aid of the ship-carpenters, John Weeks and Johann Koaster, we had laid the keel of a coasting-schooner of about thirty tons.

CHAPTER VIII.

Voyage up the River.—Description of the Country.—Meeting with strange Indians.

THE Indians having informed us that above certain rapids, there was an establishment of white men, we doubted not that it was a trading post of the Northwest Company; and to make sure of it, we procured a large canoe and a guide, and set out, on the 2d of May, Messrs M'Kay, R. Stuart, Montigny, and I, with a sufficient number of hands. We first passed a lofty headland, that seemed at a distance to be detached from the main, and to which we gave the name of *Tongue Point.* Here the river gains a width of some nine or ten miles, and keeps it for about twelve miles up. The left bank, which we were coasting, being concealed by little low islands, we encamped for the night on one of them, at the village of *Wahkaykum*, to which our guide belonged.

We continued our journey on the 3d: the river narrows considerably, at about thirty miles from its mouth, and is obstructed with islands, which are thickly covered with the willow, poplar, alder, and ash. These islands are, without exception, uninhabited and uninhabitable, being nothing but swamps, and entirely overflowed in the months of June and July; as we understood from *Coalpo*, our guide, who appeared to be an intelligent man. In proportion as we advanced, we saw the high mountains capped with snow, which form the chief and majestic feature, though a stern one, of the banks of the Columbia for some distance from its mouth, recede, and give place to a country of moderate elevation, and rising amphitheatrically from the margin of the stream. The river narrows to a mile or thereabouts; the forest is less dense, and patches of green prairie are seen. We passed a large village on the south bank, called *Kreluit*, above which is a fine forest of oaks; and encamped for the night, on a low point, at the foot of an isolated rock, about one hundred and fifty feet high. This rock appeared to me remarkable on account of its situation, reposing in the midst of a low and swampy ground, as if it had been dropped from the clouds, and seeming to have no connection with the neighboring mountains. On a cornice or shelving projection about thirty feet from its base, the natives of the adjacent villages deposite their dead, in canoes; and it is the same rock to which, for this reason, Lieutenant Broughton gave the name of *Mount Coffin.*

On the 4th, in the morning, we arrived at a large village of the same name as that which we had passed the evening before, *Kreluit*, and we landed to obtain information respecting a considerable stream, which here discharges into the Columbia, and respecting its resources for the hunter and trader in furs. It comes from the north, and is called *Cowlitzk* by the natives. Mr. M'Kay embarked with Mr. de Montigny and two Indians, in a small canoe, to examine the course of this river, a certain distance up. On entering the stream, they saw a great number of birds, which they took at first for turkeys, so much they resembled them, but which were only a kind of carrion eagles, vulgarly called *turkey-buzzards*. We were not a little astonished to see Mr. de Montigny return on foot and alone; he soon informed us of the reason: having ascended the *Kowlitzk* about a mile and a half, on rounding a bend of the stream, they suddenly came in view of about twenty canoes, full of Indians, who had made a rush upon them with the most frightful yells; the two natives and the guide who conducted their little canoe, retreated with the utmost precipitancy, but seeing that they would be overtaken, they stopped short, and begged Mr. M'Kay to fire upon the approaching savages, which he, being well acquainted with the Indian character from the time he accompanied Sir Alexander M'Kenzie, and having met with similar occurrences before, would by no means do; but displayed a friendly sign to the astonished natives, and invited them to land for an amicable talk; to which they immediately assented. Mr. M'Kay had sent Mr. de Montigny to procure some tobacco and a pipe, in order to strike a peace with these barbarians. The latter then returned to Mr. M'Kay, with the necessary articles, and in the evening the party came back to our camp, which we had fixed between the villages. We were then informed that the Indians whom Mr. M'Kay had met, were at war with the *Kreluits*. It was impossible, consequently, to close our eyes all night; the natives passing and repassing continually from one village to the other, making fearful cries, and coming every minute to solicit us to discharge our firearms; all to frighten their enemies, and let them see that they were on their guard.

On the 5th, in the morning, we paid a visit to the hostile camp; and those savages, who had never seen white men, regarded us with curiosity and astonishment, lifting the legs of our trowsers and opening our shirts, to see if the skin of our bodies resembled that of our faces and hands We remained some time with them, to make pro posals of peace; and having ascertained that this warlike demonstration originated in a trifling offence on the part of the *Kreluits*, we found them well disposed to arrange matters in an amicable fashion. After having given them, therefore, some looking-glasses, beads, knives, tobacco, and other trifles, we quitted them and pursued our way.

Having passed a deserted village, and then several islands, we came in sight of a noble mountain on the north, about twenty miles distant, all covered with snow, contrasting remarkably with the dark foliage of the forests at its base, and probably the same which was seen by Broughton, and named by him *Mount St. Helen's*. We pulled against a strong current all this day, and at evening our guide made us enter a little river, on the bank of which we found a good camping place, under a grove of oaks, and in the midst of odoriferous wild flowers, where we passed a night more tranquil than that which had preceded it.

On the morning of the 6th we ascended this small

stream, and soon arrived at a large village called *Thlakalamah*, the chief whereof, who was a young and handsome man, was called *Keasseno*, and was a relative of our guide. The situation of this village is the most charming that can be, being built on the little river that we had ascended, and indeed at its navigable head, being here but a torrent with numerous cascades leaping from rock to rock in their descent to the deep, limpid water, which then flows through a beautiful prairie, enamelled with odorous flowers of all colors, and studded with superb groves of oak. The freshness and beauty of this spot, which Nature seemed to have taken pleasure in adorning and enriching with her most precious gifts, contrasted, in a striking manner, with the indigence and uncleanliness of its inhabitants; and I regretted that it had not fallen to the lot of civilized men. I was wrong no doubt: it is just that those should be most favored by their common mother, who are least disposed to pervert her gifts, or to give the preference to advantages which are factitious, and often very frivolous. We quitted witn regret this charming spot, and soon came to another large village, which our guide informed us was called *Kathlapootle*, and was situated at the confluence of a small stream, that seemed to flow down from the mountain covered with snow, which we had seen the day before: this river is called *Cowilkt*. We coasted a pretty island, well timbered, and high enough above the level of the Columbia to escape inundation in the freshets, and arrived at two villages called *Maltnabah*. We then passed the confluence of the river *Wallamat*, or *Willamet*, above which the tide ceases to be felt in the Columbia. Our guide informed us that ascending this river about a day's journey, there was a considerable fall, beyond which the country abounded in deer, elk, bear, beaver, and otter. But here, at the spot where we were; the oaks and poplar which line both banks of the river, the green and flowery prairies discerned through the trees, and the mountains discovered in the distance, offer to the eye of the observer who loves the beauties of simple nature, a prospect the most lovely and enchanting. We encamped for the night on the edge of one of these fine prairies.

On the 7th we passed several low islands, and soon discovered *Mount Hood*, a high mountain, capped with snow, so named by Lieutenant Broughton; and *Mount Washington*, another snowy summit, so called by Lewis and Clarke. The prospect which the former had before his eyes at this place, appeared to him so charming, that landing upon a point, to take possession of the country in the name of King George, he named it *Pointe Belle Vue*. At two o'clock we passed *Point Vancouver*, the highest reached by Broughton. The width of the river diminishes considerably above this point, and we began very soon to encounter shoals of sand and gravel; a sure indication that we were nearing the rapids. We encamped that evening under a ledge of rocks, descending almost to the water's edge.

The next day, the 8th, we did not proceed far before we encountered a very rapid current. Soon after, we saw a hut of Indians engaged in fishing, where we stopped to breakfast. We found here an old blind man, who gave us a cordial reception. Our guide said that he was a white man, and that his name was *Soto*. We learned from the mouth of the old man himself, that he was the son of a Spaniard who had been wrecked at the mouth of the river; that a part of the crew on this occasion got safe ashore, but were all massacred by the Clatsops, with the exception of four, who were spared and who married native women; that these four Spaniards, of whom his father was one, disgusted with the savage life, attempted to reach a settlement of their own nation toward the south, but had never been heard of since; and that when his father, with his companions, left the country, he himself was yet quite young.* These good people having regaled us with fresh salmon, we left them, and arrived very soon at a rapid, opposite an island, named *Strawberry Island* by Captains Lewis and

* These facts, if they were authenticated, would prove that the Spaniards were the first who discovered the mouth of the Columbia. It is certain that long before the voyages of Captains Gray and Vancouver, they knew at least a part of the course of that river, which was designated in their maps under the name of *Oregon*.

Clarke, in 1806. We left our men at a large village, to take care of the canoe and baggage; and following our guide, after walking about two hours, in a beaten path, we came to the foot of the fall, where we amused ourselves for some time with shooting the seals, which were here in abundance, and in watching the Indians taking salmon below the cataract, in their scoop-nets, from stages erected for that purpose over the eddies. A chief, a young man of fine person and a good mien, came to us, followed by some twenty others, and invited us to his wigwam: we accompanied him, had roasted salmon for supper, and some mats were spread for our night's repose.

The next morning, having ascertained that there was no trading post near the Falls, and Coalpo absolutely refusing to proceed further, alleging that the natives of the villages beyond were his enemies, and would not fail to kill him if they had him in their power, we decided to return to the encampment. Having, therefore, distributed some presents to our host (I mean the young chief with whom we had supped and lodged) and to some of his followers, and procured a supply of fresh salmon for the return voyage, we re-embarked and reached the camp on the 14th, without accidents or incidents worth relating.

CHAPTER IX.

Departure of the Tonquin.—Indian Messengers.—Project of an Expedition to the Interior.—Arrival of Mr. Daniel Thompson.—Departure of the Expedition.—Designs upon us by the Natives.—Rumors of the Destruction of the Tonquin.—Scarcity of Provisions.—Narrative of a strange Indian.—Duplicity and Cunning of Comcomly.

HAVING built a warehouse (62 feet by 20) to put under cover the articles we were to receive from the ship, we were busily occupied, from the 16th to the 30th, in stowing away the goods and other effects intended for the establishment.

The ship, which had been detained by circumstances, much longer than had been anticipated, left her anchorage at last, on the 1st of June, and dropped down to Baker's bay, there to wait for a favorable wind to get out of the river. As she was to coast along the north, and enter all the harbors, in order to procure as many furs as possible, and to touch at the Columbia river before she finally left these seas for the United States, it was unanimously resolved among the partners, that Mr. M'Kay should join the cruise, as well to aid the captain, as to obtain correct information in regard to the commerce with the natives on that coast. Mr. M'Kay selected Messrs. J. Lewis and O. de Montigny to accompany him; but the latter having represented that the sea made him sick, was excused; and Mr. M'Kay shipped in his place a young man named Louis Buslé, to serve him in the capacity of domestic, being one of the young Canadian sailors. I had the good fortune not to be chosen for this disastrous voyage, thanks to my having made myself useful at the establishment. Mr. Mumford (the second mate) owed the same happiness to the incompatibility of his disposition with that of the captain; he had permission to remain, and engaged with the company in place of Mr. Aikin as coaster, and in command of the schooner.*

* This schooner was found too small for the purpose. Mr. Astor had no idea of the dangers to be met at the mouth of the

On the 5th of June, the ship got out to sea, with a good wind. We continued in the mean time to labor without intermission at the completion of the storehouse, and in the erection of a dwelling for ourselves, and a powder magazine. These buildings were constructed of hewn logs, and, in the absence of boards, tightly covered and roofed with cedar bark. The natives, of both sexes, visited us more frequently, and formed a pretty considerable camp near the establishment.

On the 15th, some natives from up the river, brought us two strange Indians, a man and a woman. They were not attired like the savages on the river Columbia, but wore long robes of dressed deer-skin, with leggings and moccasins in the fashion of the tribes to the east of the Rocky Mountains. We put questions to them in various Indian dialects; but they did not understand us. They showed us a letter addressed to

Columbia, or he would have ordered the frame of a vessel of at least one hundred tons. The frames shipped in New York were used in the construction of this one only, which was employed solely in the river trade.

" *Mr. John Stuart, Fort Estekatadene, New Caledonia.*" Mr. Pillet then addressing them in the *Knisteneaux* language, they answered, although they appeared not to understand it perfectly. Notwithstanding, we learned from them that they had been sent by a Mr. Finnan M'Donald, a clerk in the service of the Northwest Company, and who had a post on a river which they called *Spokan;* that having lost their way, they had followed the course of the *Tacousah-Tesseh* (the Indian name of the Columbia), that when they arrived at the Falls, the natives made them understand that there were white men at the mouth of the river; and not doubting that the person to whom the letter was addressed would be found there, they had come to deliver it.

We kept these messengers for some days, and having drawn from them important information respecting the country in the interior, west of the Mountains, we decided to send an expedition thither, under the command of Mr. David Stuart; and the 15th July was fixed for its departure.

All was in fact ready on the appointed day,

and we were about to load the canoes, when toward midday, we saw a large canoe, with a flag displayed at her stern, rounding the point which we called *Tongue Point.* We knew not who it could be; for we did not so soon expect our own party, who (as the reader will remember) were to cross the continent, by the route which Captains Lewis and Clarke had followed, in 1805, and to winter for that purpose somewhere on the Missouri. We were soon relieved of our uncertainty by the arrival of the canoe, which touched shore at a little wharf that we had built to facilitate the landing of goods from the vessel. The flag she bore was the British, and her crew was composed of eight Canadian boatmen or *voyageurs.* A well-dressed man, who appeared to be the commander, was the first to leap ashore, and addressing us without ceremony, said that his name was David Thompson, and that he was one of the partners of the Northwest Company. We invited him to our quarters, which were at one end of the warehouse, the dwelling-house not being yet completed. After the usual civilities had been extended to our visitor, Mr. Thompson said that he had crossed the continent during the preceding season; but that the desertion of a portion of his men had compelled him to winter at the base of the Rocky mountains, at the head waters of the Columbia. In the spring he had built a canoe, the materials for which he had brought with him across the mountains, and had come down the river to our establishment. He added that the wintering partners had resolved to abandon all their trading posts west of the mountains, not to enter into competition with us, provided our company would engage not to encroach upon their commerce on the east side: and to support what he said, produced a letter to that effect, addressed by the wintering partners to the chief of their house in Canada, the Hon. William M'Gillivray.

Mr. Thompson kept a regular journal, and travelled, I thought, more like a geographer than a fur-trader. He was provided with a sextant, chronometer and barometer, and during a week's sojourn which he made at our place, had an opportunity to make several astronomical observations. He recognised the two Indians who had brought the letter addressed to Mr. J. Stuart, and told us that they were two women, one of whom had dressed herself as a man, to travel with more security. The description which he gave us of the interior of the country was not calculated to give us a very favorable idea of it, and did not perfectly accord with that of our two Indian guests. We persevered, however, in the resolution we had taken, of sending an expedition thither; and, on the 23d Mr. D. Stuart set out, accompanied by Messrs. Pillet, Ross, M'Clellan and de Montigny, with four Canadian *voyageurs*, and the two Indian women, and in company with Mr. Thompson and his crew. The wind being favorable, the little flotilla hoisted sail, and was soon out of our sight.*

* Mr. Thompson had no doubt been sent by the agents of the Northwest Company, to take possession of an eligible spot at the mouth of the Columbia, with a view of forestalling the plan of Mr. Astor. He would have been there before us, no doubt, but for the desertion of his men. The consequence of this step would have been his taking possession of the country, and displaying the British flag, as an emblem of that possession and a guarantee

The natives, who till then had surrounded us in great numbers, began to withdraw, and very soon we saw no more of them. At first we attributed their absence to the want of furs to trade with; but we soon learned that they acted in that manner from another motive. One of the secondary chiefs who had formed a friendship for Mr. R. Stuart, informed him, that seeing us reduced in number by the expedition lately sent off, they had formed the design of surprising us, to take our lives and plunder the post. We hastened, therefore, to put ourselves in the best possible state of defence. The dwelling house was raised, parallel to the warehouse; we cut a great quantity of pickets in the forest, and formed a square, with palisades in front and rear, of about 90 feet by 120; the warehouse, built on the edge of a ravine, formed one flank, the dwelling house and shops the other; with a little bas-

of protection hereafter. He found himself too late, however, and the stars and stripes floating over *Astoria*. This note is not intended by the author as an after-thought: as the opinion it conveys was that which we all entertained at the time of that gentleman's visit.

tion at each angle north and south, on which were mounted four small cannon. The whole was finished in six days, and had a sufficiently formidable aspect to deter the Indians from attacking us ; and for greater surety, we organized a guard for day and night.

Toward the end of the month, a large assemblage of Indians from the neighborhood of the straits *Juan de Fuca*, and *Gray's Harbor*, formed a great camp on Baker's Bay, for the ostensible object of fishing for sturgeon. It was bruited among these Indians that the Tonquin had been destroyed on the coast, and Mr. M'Kay (or the chief trader, as they called him) and all the crew, massacred by the natives. We did not give credence to this rumor. Some days after, other Indians from Gray's Harbor, called *Tchikeylis*, confirmed what the first had narrated, and even gave us, as far as we could judge by the little we knew of their language, a very circumstantial detail of the affair, so that without wholly convincing us, it did not fail to make a painful impression on our minds, and keep us in an excited state of feeling as to the truth of the report. The Indians of the Bay looked fiercer and more warlike than those of our neighborhood; so we redoubled our vigilance, and performed a regular daily drill to accustom ourselves to the use of arms.

To the necessity of securing ourselves against an attack on the part of the natives, was joined that of obtaining a stock of provisions for the winter: those which we had received from the vessel were very quickly exhausted, and from the commencement of the month of July we were forced to depend upon fish. Not having brought hunters with us, we had to rely for venison, on the precarious hunt of one of the natives who had not abandoned us when the rest of his countrymen retired. This man brought us from time to time, a very lean and very dry doe-elk, for which we had to pay, notwithstanding, very dear. The ordinary price of a stag was a blanket, a knife, some tobacco, powder and ball, besides supplying our hunter with a musket. This dry meat, and smoke-dried fish, constituted our daily food, and that in very insufficient quantity for hardworking men. We had no bread, and vegetables, of course, were quite out of the question. In a word our fare was not sumptuous. Those who accommodated themselves best to our mode of living were the Sandwich-islanders: salmon and elk were to them exquisite viands.

On the 11th of August a number of Chinooks visited us, bringing a strange Indian, who had, they said, something interesting to communicate. This savage told us, in fact, that he had been engaged with ten more of his countrymen, by a Captain *Ayres*, to hunt seals on the islands in *Sir Francis Drake's Bay*, where these animals are very numerous, with a promise of being taken home and paid for their services; the captain had left them on the islands, to go southwardly and purchase provisions, he said, of the Spaniards of Monterey in California; but he had never returned: and they, believing that he had been wrecked, had embarked in a skiff which he had left them, and had reached the main land, from which they were not far distant; but their skiff was shattered to pieces in the surf, and they had saved themselves by swimming. Believing that they were not far from the river Columbia, they had followed the shore, living, on the way, upon shell-fish and frogs; at last they arrived among strange Indians, who, far from receiving them kindly, had killed eight of them and made the rest prisoners; but the *Klemooks*, a neighboring tribe to the *Clatsops*, hearing that they were captives, had ransomed them.

These facts must have occurred in March or April, 1811. The Indian who gave us an account of them, appeared to have a great deal of intelligence and knew some words of the English language. He added that he had been at the Russian trading post at *Chitka*, that he had visited the coast of California, the Sandwich islands, and even China.

About this time, old Comcomly sent to *Astoria* for Mr. Stuart and me, to come and cure him of a swelled throat, which, he said, afflicted him sorely. As it was late in the day, we postponed till to-morrow going to cure the chief of the Chinooks; and it was well we did; for, the same evening, the wife of the Indian who had accompanied us in our voyage to the Falls, sent us word that Comcomly was perfectly well, the pretended *tonsillitis* being only a pretext to get us in his power. This timely advice kept us at home.

CHAPTER X.

Occupations at Astoria.—Return of a Portion of the Men of the Expedition to the Interior.—New Expedition.—Excursion in Search of three Deserters.

On the 26th of September our house was finished, and we took possession of it. The mason work had at first caused us some difficulty; but at last, not being able to make lime for want of lime-stones, we employed blue clay as a substitute for mortar. This dwelling-house was sufficiently spacious to hold all our company, and we had distributed it in the most convenient manner that we could. It comprised a sitting, a dining room, some lodging or sleeping rooms, and an apartment for the men and artificers, all under the same roof. We also completed a shop for the blacksmith, who till that time had worked in the open air.

The schooner, the construction of which had necessarily languished for want of an adequate force at the ship-yard, was finally launched on the 2d of October, and named the *Dolly*, with the formalities usual on such occasions. I was on that day at *Young's Bay*, where I saw the ruins of the quarters erected by Captains Lewis and Clarke, in 1805–'06: they were but piles of rough, unhewn logs, overgrown with parasite creepers.

On the evening of the 5th, Messrs. Pillet and M'Lellan arrived, from the party of Mr. David Stuart, in a canoe manned by two of his men. They brought, as passengers, Mr. Régis Bruguier, whom I had known in Canada as a respectable country merchant, and an Iroquois family. Mr. Bruguier had been a trader among the Indians on the Saskatchewine river, where he had lost his outfit: he had since turned trapper, and had come into this region to hunt beaver, being provided with traps and other needful implements. The report which these gentlemen gave of the interior was highly satisfactory: they had found the climate salubrious, and had been well received by the natives. The latter possessed a great number of horses, and Mr. Stuart had purchased several of these animals at a low price. Ascending the river they had come to a pretty stream, which the natives called *Okenakan*. Mr. Stuart had resolved to establish his post on the bank of this river, and having erected a log-house, he thought best to send back the above named persons, retaining with him, for the winter, only Messrs. Ross and de Montigny, and two men.*

Meanwhile, the season being come when the Indians quit the seashore and the banks of the Columbia, to retire into the woods and establish their winter quarters along the small streams and rivers, we began to find ourselves short of provisions, having received no supplies from them for some time. It was therefore determined that Mr. R. Stuart should set out in the schooner with

* One of these men had been left with him by Mr. Thompson, in exchange for a Sandwich-islander whom that gentleman proposed to take to Canada, and thence to England.

Mr. Mumford, for the threefold purpose, of obtaining all the provisions they could, cutting oaken staves for the use of the cooper, and trading with the Indians up the river. They left with this design on the 12th. At the end of five days Mr. Mumford returned in a canoe of Indians. This man having wished to assume the command, and to order (in the style of Captain Thorn) the person who had engaged him to obey, had been sent back in consequence to *Astoria*.

On the 10th of November we discovered that three of our people had absconded, viz., P. D. Jeremie, and the two Belleaux. They had leave to go out shooting for two days, and carried off with them firearms and ammunition, and a handsome light Indian canoe. As soon as their flight was known, having procured a large canoe of the Chinooks, we embarked, Mr. Matthews and I, with five natives, to pursue them, with orders to proceed as far as the Falls, if necessary. On the 11th, having ascended the river to a place called *Oak Point*, we overtook the schooner lying at anchor, while Mr. Stuart was taking in a load of staves and hoop-poles. Mr. Farnham joined our party, as well as one of the hands, and thus reinforced, we pursued our way, journeying day and night, and stopping at every Indian village, to make inquiries and offer a reward for the apprehension of our runaways. Having reached the Falls without finding any trace of them, and our provisions giving out, we retraced our steps, and arrived on the 16th at Oak Point, which we found Mr. Stuart ready to quit.

Meanwhile, the natives of the vicinity informed us that they had seen the marks of shoes imprinted on the sand, at the confluence of a small stream in the neighborhood. We got three small canoes, carrying two persons each, and having ascertained that the information was correct, after searching the environs during a part of the 17th, we ascended the small stream as far as some high lands which are seen from Oak Point, and which lie about eight or nine miles south of it. The space between these high lands and the ridge crowned with oaks on the bank of the Columbia, is a low and swampy land, cut up by an infinity of little channels. Toward evening we returned on our path, to regain the schooner; but instead of taking the circuitous way of the river, by which we had come, we made for Oak Point by the most direct route, through these channels; but night coming on, we lost ourselves. Our situation became the most disagreeable that can be imagined. Being unable to find a place where we could land, on account of the morass, we were obliged to continue rowing, or rather turning round, in this species of labyrinth, constantly kneeling in our little canoes, which any unlucky movement would infallibly have caused to upset. It rained in torrents and was dark as pitch. At last, after having wandered about during a considerable part of the night, we succeeded in gaining the edge of the mainland. Leaving there our canoes, because we could not drag them (as we attempted) through the forest, we crossed the woods in the darkness, tearing ourselves with the brush, and reached the schooner, at about two in the morning, benumbed with cold and exhausted with fatigue.

The 18th was spent in getting in the remainder of the lading of the little vessel, and on the morning of the 19th we raised anchor, and dropped down abreast of the Kreluit village, where some of the Indians offering to aid us in the search after our deserters, Mr. Stuart put Mr. Farnham and me on shore to make another attempt. We passed that day in drying our clothes, and the next day embarked in a canoe, with one *Kreluit* man and a squaw, and ascended the river before described as entering the Columbia at this place. We soon met a canoe of natives, who informed us that our runaways had been made prisoners by the chief of a tribe which dwells upon the banks of the Willamet river, and which they called *Cathlanaminim*. We kept on and encamped on a beach of sand opposite *Deer island*. There we passed a night almost as disagreeable as that of the 17th–18th. We had lighted a fire, and contrived a shelter of mats; but there came on presently a violent gust of wind, accompanied with a heavy rain: our fire was put out, our mats were carried away, and we could neither rekindle the one nor find the others: so that we had to remain all night exposed to the fury of the storm. As soon as it was day we re-embarked, and set ourselves to paddling with all our might to warm ourselves. In the evening we arrived near the village where our deserters were, and saw one of them on the skirts of it. We proceeded to the hut of the chief, where we found all three, more inclined to follow us than to remain as slaves among these barbarians. We passed the night in the chief's lodge, not without some fear and some precaution; this chief having the reputation of being a wicked man, and capable of violating the rights of parties. He was a man of high stature and a good mien, and proud in proportion, as we discovered by the chilling and haughty manner in which he received us. Farnham and I agreed to keep watch alternately, but this arrangement was superfluous, as neither of us could sleep a wink for the infernal thumping and singing made by the medicine men all night long, by a dying native. I had an opportunity of seeing the sick man make his last will and testament: having caused to be brought to him whatever he had that was most precious, his bracelets of copper, his bead necklace, his bow and arrows and quiver, his nets, his lines, his spear, his pipe, &c., he distributed the whole to his most intimate friends, with a promise on their part, to restore them, if he recovered.

On the 22d, after a great deal of talk, and infinite quibbling on the part of the chief, we agreed with him for the ransom of our men. I had visited every lodge in the village and found but few of the young men, the greater part having gone on a fishing excursion; knowing, therefore, that the chief could not be supported by his warriors, I was resolved not be imposed upon, and as I knew where the firearms of the fugitives had been deposited, I would have them at all hazards; but we were obliged to give him all our blankets, amounting to eight, a brass kettle, a hatchet, a small pistol, much out of order, a powder-horn, and some rounds of ammunition: with these articles placed in a pile before him, we demanded the men's clothing, the three fowling-pieces, and their canoe, which he had caused to be hidden in the woods. Nothing but our firmness compelled him to accept the articles offered in exchange; but at last, with great reluctance, he closed the bargain, and suffered us to depart in the evening with the prisoners and the property.

We all five (including the three deserters) embarked in the large canoe, leaving our Kreluit and his wife to follow in the other, and proceeded as far as the Cowlitzk, where we camped. The next day, we pursued our journey homeward, only stopping at the Kreluit village to get some provisions, and soon entered the group of islands which crowd the river above Gray's bay. On one of these we stopped to amuse ourselves with shooting some ducks, and meanwhile a smart breeze springing up, we split open a double-rush mat (which had served as a bag), to make a sail, and having cut a forked sapling for a mast, shipped a few boulders to stay the foot of it, and spread our canvass to the wind. We soon arrived in sight of Gray's bay, at a distance of fourteen or fifteen miles from our establishment.

We had, notwithstanding, a long passage across, the river forming in this place, as I have before observed, a sort of lake, by the recession of its shores on either hand: but the wind was fair. We undertook, then, to cross, and quitted the island, to enter the broad, lake-like expanse, just as the sun was going down, hoping to reach Astoria in a couple of hours.

We were not long before we repented of our temerity: for in a short time the sky became overcast, the wind increased till it blew with violence, and meeting with the tide, caused the waves to rise prodigiously, which broke over our wretched canoe, and filled it with water. We lightened it as much as we could, by throwing overboard the little baggage we had left, and I set the men to baling with our remaining brass kettle. At last, after having been, for three hours, the sport of the raging billows, and threatened every instant with being swallowed up, we had the unexpected happiness of landing in a cove on the north shore of the river. Our first care was to thank the Almighty for having delivered us from so imminent a danger. Then, when we had secured the canoe, and groped our way to the forest, where we made, with branches of trees, a shelter against the wind—still continuing to blow with violence, and kindled a great fire to warm us and dry our clothes. That did not prevent us from shivering the rest of the night, even in congratulating ourselves on the happiness of setting our foot on shore at the moment when we began quite to despair of saving ourselves at all.

The morning of the 24th brought with it a clear sky, but no abatement in the violence of the wind, till toward evening, when we again embarked, and arrived with our deserters at the establishment, where they never expected to see us again. Some Indians who had followed us in a canoe, up to the moment when we undertook the passage across the evening before, had followed the southern shore, and making the portage of the isthmus of Tongue Point, had happily arrived at Astoria. These natives, not doubting that we were lost, so reported us to Mr M'Dougal; accordingly that gentleman was equally overjoyed and astonished at beholding us safely landed, which procured, not only for us, but for the culprits, our companions, a cordial and hearty reception.

CHAPTER XI.

Departure of Mr. R. Stuart for the Interior.—Occupations at Astoria.—Arrival of Messrs. Donald M'Kenzie and Robert M'Lellan.—Account of their Journey.—Arrival of Mr. Wilson P. Hunt.

THE natives having given us to understand that beaver was very abundant in the country watered by the Willamet, Mr. R. Stuart procured a guide, and set out, on the 5th of December, accompanied by Messrs. Pillet and M'Gillis and a few of the men, to ascend that river and ascertain whether or no it would be advisable to establish a trading-post on its banks. Mr. R. Bruguier accompanied them to follow his pursuits as a trapper.

The season at which we expected the return of the Tonquin was now past, and we began to regard as too probable the report of the Indians of Gray's Harbor. We still flattered ourselves, notwithstanding, with the hope that perhaps that vessel had sailed for the East Indies, without touching at Astoria; but this was at most a conjecture.

The 25th, Christmas-day, passed very agreeably: we treated the men, on that day, with the best the establishment afforded. Although that was no great affair, they seemed well satisfied; for they had been restricted, during the last few months, to a very meagre diet, living, as one may say, on sun-dried fish. On the 27th, the schooner having returned from her second voyage up the river, we dismantled her, and laid her up for the winter at the entrance of a small creek.

The weather, which had been raining, almost without interruption, from the beginning of October, cleared up on the evening of the 31st; and the 1st January, 1812, brought us a clear and serene sky. We proclaimed the new year with a discharge of artillery. A small allowance of spirits was served to the men, and the day passed in gayety, every one amusing himself as well as he could.

The festival over, our people resumed their ordinary occupations: while some cut timber for building, and others made charcoal for the blacksmith, the carpenter constructed a barge, and the cooper made barrels for the use of the posts we proposed to establish in the interior. On the 18th, in the evening, two canoes full of white men arrived at the establishment. Mr. M'Dougal, the resident agent, being confined to his room by sickness, the duty of receiving the strangers devolved on me. My astonishment was not slight, when one of the party called me by name, as he extended his hand, and I recognised Mr. Donald M'Kenzie, the same who had quitted Montreal, with Mr. W. P. Hunt, in the month of July, 1810. He was accompanied by a Mr. Robert M'Lellan, a partner, Mr. John Reed, a clerk, and eight *voyageurs*, or boatmen. After having reposed themselves a little from their fatigues, these gentlemen recounted to us the history of their journey, of which the following is the substance.

Messrs. Hunt and M'Kenzie, quitting Canada,

proceeded by way of Mackinac and St. Louis, and ascended the Missouri, in the autumn of 1810, to a place on that river called *Nadoway*, where they wintered. Here they were joined by Mr. R. M'Lellan, by a Mr. Crooks, and a Mr. Müller, traders with the Indians of the South, and all having business relations with Mr. Astor.

In the spring of 1811, having procured two large keel-boats, they ascended the Missouri to the country of the *Arikaras*, or Rice Indians, where they disposed of their boats and a great part of their luggage, to a Spanish trader, by name *Manuel Lisa*. Having purchased of him, and among the Indians, 130 horses, they resumed their route, in the beginning of August, to the number of some sixty-five persons, to proceed across the mountains to the river Columbia. Wishing to avoid the *Blackfeet* Indians, a warlike and ferocious tribe, who put to death all the strangers that fall into their hands, they directed their course southwardly, until they arrived at the 40th degree of latitude. Thence they turned to the northwest, and arrived, by-and-by, at an old fort, or trading post, on the banks of a little river flowing west. This post, which was then deserted, had been established, as they afterward learned, by a trader named Henry. Our people, not doubting that this stream would conduct them to the Columbia, and finding it navigable, constructed some canoes to descend it. Having left some hunters (or trappers) near the old fort, with Mr. Miller, who, dissatisfied with the expedition, was resolved to return to the United States, the party embarked; but very soon finding the river obstructed with rapids and waterfalls, after having upset some of the canoes, lost one man by drowning, and also a part of their baggage, perceiving that the stream was impracticable, they resolved to abandon their canoes and proceed on foot. The enterprise was one of great difficulty, considering the small stock of provisions they had left. Nevertheless, as there was no time to lose in deliberation, after depositing in a *cache* the superflous part of their baggage, they divided themselves into four companies, under the command of Messrs. M'Kenzie, Hunt, M'Lellan and Crooks, and proceeded to follow the course of the stream, which they named *Mad river*, on account of the insurmountable difficulties it presented. Messrs. M'Kenzie and M'Lellan took the right bank, and Messrs. Hunt and Crook the left. They counted on arriving very quickly at the Columbia; but they followed this Mad river for twenty days, finding nothing at all to eat, and suffering horribly from thirst. The rocks between which the river flows being so steep and abrupt as to prevent their descending to quench their thirst (so that even their dogs died of it), they suffered the torments of Tantalus, with this difference, that he had the water which he could not reach above his head, while our travellers had it beneath their feet. Several, not to die of this raging thirst, drank their own urine: all, to appease the cravings of hunger, ate beaver skins roasted in the evening at the camp-fire. They even were at last constrained to eat their moccasins. Those on the left, or southeast bank, suffered, however, less than the others, because they occasionally fell in with Indians, utterly wild indeed, and who fled at their approach, carrying off their horses. According to all appearances these savages had never seen white men. Our travellers, when they arrived in sight of the camp of one of these wandering hordes, approached it with as much precaution, and with the same stratagem that they would have used with a troop of wild beasts. Having thus surprised them, they would fire upon the horses, some of which would fall; but they took care to leave some trinkets on the spot, to indemnify the owners for what they had taken from them by violence. This resource prevented the party from perishing of hunger.

Mr. M'Kenzie having overtaken Mr. M'Lellan, their two companies pursued the journey together. Very soon after this junction, they had an opportunity of approaching sufficiently near to Mr. Hunt, who, as I have remarked, was on the other bank, to speak to him, and inform him of their distressed state. Mr. Hunt caused a canoe to be made of a horse-hide; it was not, as one may suppose, very large; but they succeeded, nevertheless, by that means, in conveying a little horse-flesh to the people on the north bank. It was attempted, even, to pass them across, one by one (for the skiff would not hold any more); several had actually crossed to the south side, when, unhappily, owing to the impetuosity of the current, the canoe capsized, a man was drowned, and the two parties lost all hope of being able to unite. They continued their route, therefore, each on their own side of the river. In a short time those upon the north bank came to a more considerable stream, which they followed down. They also met, very opportunely, some Indians, who sold them a number of horses. They also encountered, in these parts, a young American, who was deranged, but who sometimes recovered his reason. This young man told them, in one of his lucid intervals, that he was from Connecticut, and was named Archibald Pelton; that he had come up the Missouri with Mr. Henry; that all the people at the post established by that trader were massacred by the Blackfeet; that he alone had escaped, and had been wandering, for three years since, with the *Snake* Indians.* Our people took this young man with them. Arriving at the confluence with the Columbia, of the river whose banks they were following, they perceived that it was the same which had been called *Lewis river*, by the American captain of that name, in 1805. Here, then, they exchanged their remaining horses for canoes, and so arrived at the establishment, safe and sound, it is true, but in a pitiable condition to see; their clothes being nothing but fluttering rags.

The narrative of these gentlemen interested us very much. They added, that since their separation from Messrs. Hunt and Crooks, they had neither seen nor heard aught of them, and believed it impossible that they should arrive at the establishment before spring. They were mistaken, however, for Mr. Hunt arrived on the

* A thoroughly savage and lazy tribe, inhabiting the plains of the Columbia, between the 43d and 44th degrees of latitude.

15th February, with thirty men, one woman, and two children, having left Mr. Crooks, with five men, among the *Snakes*. They might have reached Astoria almost as soon as Mr. M'Kenzie, but they had passed from eight to ten days in the midst of a plain, among some friendly Indians, as well to recruit their strength, as to make search for two of the party, who had been lost in the woods. Not finding them, they had resumed their journey, and struck the banks of the Columbia a little lower down than the mouth of Lewis river, where Mr. M'Kenzie had come out.

The arrival of so great a number of persons would have embarrassed us, had it taken place a month sooner. Happily, at this time, the natives were bringing in fresh fish in abundance. Until the 30th of March, we were occupied in preparing triplicates of letters and other necessary papers, in order to send Mr. Astor the news of our arrival, and of the reunion of the two expeditions. The letters were intrusted to Mr. John Reed, who quitted Astoria for St. Louis, in company with Mr. M'Lellan—another discontented partner, who wished to disconnect himself with the association,—and Mr. R. Stuart, who was conveying two canoe-loads of goods for his uncle's post on the *Okenakan.* Messrs. Farnham and M'Gillis set out at the same time, with a guide, and were instructed to proceed to the *cache*,* where the overland travellers had

* These *caches* are famous in all the narratives of overland travel, whether for trade or discovery. The manner of making them is described by Captains Lewis and Clarke, as follows: they choose a dry situation, then describing a circle of some twenty inches diameter, remove the sod as gently and carefully as possible. The hole is then sunk a foot deep or more, perpendicularly; it is then worked gradually wider as it descends, till it becomes six or seven feet deep, and shaped like a kettle, or the lower part of a large still. As the earth is dug out, it is handed up in a vessel, and carefully laid upon a skin or cloth, in which it is carried away, and usually thrown into the river, if there be one, or concealed so as to leave no trace of it. A floor of three or four inches thick is then made of dry sticks, on which is thrown hay or a hide perfectly dry. The goods, after being well aired and dried, are laid down, and preserved from contact with the wall by a layer of other dried sticks, till all is stowed away. When the hole is nearly full, a hide is laid on top, and the earth is thrown upon this, and beaten down, until, with the addition of the sod first removed, the whole is on a level with the ground, and there remains not the slightest appearance of an excavation. The first shower effaces every sign of what has been done, and such a cache is safe for years.—Ed.

hidden their goods, near old Fort Henry, on the Mad river. I profited by this opportunity to write to my family in Canada. Two days after, Messrs. M'Kenzie and Matthews set out, with five or six men, as hunters, to make an excursion up the Willamet river.

CHAPTER XII.

Arrival of the Ship Beaver.—Unexpected Return of Messrs. D Stuart, R. Stuart, M'Lelland, &c.—Cause of that Return.—Ship discharging.—New Expeditions.—Hostile Attitude of the Natives.—Departure of the Beaver.—Journeys of the Author.—His Occupations at the Establishment.

From the departure of the last outfit under Mr. M'Kenzie, nothing remarkable took place at Astoria, till the 9th of May. On that day we descried, to our great surprise and great joy, a sail in the offing, opposite the mouth of the river. Forthwith Mr. M'Dougal was despatched in a boat to the cape, to make the signals. On the morning of the 10th, the weather being fine and the sea smooth, the boat pushed out and arrived safely alongside. Soon after, the wind springing up, the vessel made sail and entered the river, where she dropped anchor, in Baker's Bay, at about 2 P. M. Toward evening the boat returned to the Fort, with the following passengers: Messrs. John Clarke of Canada (a wintering partner), Alfred Seton, George Ehnainger, a nephew of Mr. Astor (clerks), and two men. We learned from these gentlemen that the vessel was the *Beaver*, Captain *Cornelius Sowles*, and was consigned to us; that she left New York on the 10th of October, and had touched, in the passage, at *Massa Fuero* and the Sandwich Isles. Mr. Clarke handed me letters from my father and from several of my friends: I thus learned that death had deprived me of a beloved sister.

On the morning of the 11th, we were strangely surprised by the return of Messrs. D. Stuart, R. Stuart, R. M'Lelland, Crooks, Reed, and Farnham. This return, as sudden as unlooked for, was owing to an unfortunate adventure which befell the party, in ascending the river. When they reached the Falls, where the portage is very long, some natives came with their horses, to offer their aid in transporting the goods. Mr. R. Stuart, not distrusting them, confided to their care some bales of merchandise, which they packed on their horses: but, in making the transit, they darted up a narrow path among the rocks, and fled at full gallop toward the prairie, without its being possible to overtake them. Mr. Stuart had several shots fired over their heads, to frighten them, but it had no other effect than to increase their speed. Meanwhile our own people continued the transportation of the rest of the goods, and of the canoes; but as there was a great number of natives about, whom the success and impunity of those thieves had emboldened, Mr. Stuart thought it prudent to keep watch over the goods at the upper end of the portage, while Messrs. M'Lellan and Reed made the rear-guard. The last named gentleman, who carried, strapped to his shoulders, a tin box containing the letters and despatches for New York with which he was charged, happened to be at some distance from the former, and the Indians thought it a favorable opportunity to attack him and carry off his box, the brightness of which no doubt had tempted their cupidity. They threw themselves upon him so suddenly that he had no time to place himself on the defensive. After a short resistance, he received a blow on the head from a war club, which felled him to the ground, and the Indians seized upon their booty. Mr. M'Lellan perceiving what was done, fired his carabine at one of the robbers and made him bite the dust; the rest took to flight, but carried off the box notwithstanding. Mr. M'Lellan immediately ran up to Mr. Reed; but finding the latter motionless and bathed in blood, he hastened to rejoin Mr. Stuart, urging him to get away from these robbers and murderers. But Mr. Stuart, being a self-possessed and fearless man, would not proceed without ascertaining if Mr. Reed were really dead, or if he were, without carrying off his body; and notwithstanding the remonstrances of Mr. M'Lellan, taking his way back to the spot where the latter had left his companion, had not gone two hundred paces, when he met him coming toward them, holding his bleeding head with both hands.*

* We were apprized of this unfortunate rencontre by natives from up the river, on the 15th of April, but disbelieved it. [It is

The object of Mr. Reed's journey being defeated by the loss of his papers, he repaired, with the other gentlemen, to Mr. David Stuart's trading post, at Okenakan, whence they had all set out, in the beginning of May, to returu to Astoria. Coming down the river, they fell in with Mr. R. Crooks, and a man named *John Day*. It was observed in the preceding chapter that Mr. Crooks remained with five men among some Indians who were there termed *friendly:* but this gentleman and his companion were the only members of that party who ever reached the establishment: and they too arrived in a most pitiable condition, the savages having stripped

curious to observe the want of military sagacity and precaution which characterized the operations of these traders, compared with the exact calculations of danger and the unfailing measures of defence, employed from the very outset by Captains Lewis and Clarke in the same country. There was one very audacious attempt at plunder made upon the latter; but besides that it cost the Indians a life or two, the latter lost property of their own far exceeding their booty. It is true that the American officers had a stronger force at their disposal than our merchants had, and that, too, consisting of experienced western hunters and veteran soldiers of the frontier; but it is not less interesting to note the difference, because it is easy to account for it.—J. V. H.]

them of everything, leaving them but some bits of deerskin to cover their nakedness.

On the 12th, the schooner, which had been sent down the river to the Beaver's anchorage, returned with a cargo (being the stores intended for Astoria), and the following passengers: to wit, Messrs. B. Clapp, J. C. Halsey, C. A. Nichols, and R. Cox, clerks; five Canadians, seven Americans (all mechanics), and a dozen Sandwich-islanders for the service of the establishment. The captain of the Beaver sounded the channel diligently for several days; but finding it scarcely deep enough for so large a vessel, he was unwilling to bring her up to Astoria. It was necessary, in consequence, to use the schooner as a lighter in discharging the ship, and this tedious operation occupied us during the balance of this month and a part of June.

Captain Sowles and Mr. Clarke confirmed the report of the destruction of the Tonquin; they had learned it at Owhyhee, by means of a letter which a certain Captain Ebbetts, in the employ of Mr. Astor, had left there. It was nevertheless resolved that Mr. Hunt should embark upon the "Beaver," to carry out the plan of an exact commercial survey of the coast, which Mr. M'Kay had been sent to accomplish, and in particular to visit for that purpose the Russian establishments at Chitka sound.

The necessary papers having been prepared anew, and being now ready to expedite, were confided to Mr. R. Stuart, who was to cross the continent in company with Messrs. Crooks and R. M'Lellan, partners dissatisfied with the enterprise, and who had made up their minds to return to the United States. Mr. Clark, accompanied by Messrs. Pillet, Donald, M'Lellan, Farnham and Cox, was fitted out at the same time, with a considerable assortment of merchandise, to form a new establishment on the *Spokan* or Clarke's river. Mr. M'Kenzie, with Mr. Seton, was destined for the borders of *Lewis* river: while Mr. David Stuart, reinforced by Messrs. Matthews and M'Gillis, was to explore the region lying north of his post at Okenakan. All these outfits being ready, with the canoes, boatmen, and hunters, the flotilla quitted Astoria on the 30th of June, in the afternoon, having on board sixty-two persons. The sequel will show the result of the several expeditions.

During the whole month of July, the natives (seeing us weakened no doubt by these outfits), manifested their hostile intentions so openly that we were obliged to be constantly on our guard. We constructed covered ways inside our palisades, and raised our bastions or towers another story. The alarm became so serious toward the latter end of the month that we doubled our sentries day and night, and never allowed more than two or three Indians at a time within our gates.

The Beaver was ready to depart on her coasting voyage at the end of June, and on the 1st of July Mr. Hunt went on board: but westerly winds prevailing all that month, it was not till the 4th of August that she was able to get out of the river; being due again by the end of October to leave her surplus goods and take in our furs for market.

The months of August and September were

employed in finishing a house forty-five feet by thirty, shingled and perfectly tight, as a hospital for the sick, and lodging house for the mechanics.

Experience having taught us that from the beginning of October to the end of January, provisions were brought in by the natives in very small quantity, it was thought expedient that I should proceed in the schooner, accompanied by Mr. Clapp, on a trading voyage up the river to secure a cargo of dried fish. We left Astoria on the 1st of October, with a small assortment of merchandise. The trip was highly successful: we found the game very abundant, killed a great quantity of swans, ducks, foxes, &c., and returned to Astoria on the 20th, with a part of our venison, wild fowl, and bear meat, besides seven hundred and fifty smoked salmon, a quantity of the *Wapto* root (so called by the natives), which is found a good substitute for potatoes, and four hundred and fifty skins of beaver and other animals of the furry tribe.

The encouragement derived from this excursion induced us to try a second, and I set off this time alone, that is, with a crew of five men only, and an Indian boy, son of the old chief Comcomly. This second voyage proved anything but agreeable. We experienced continual rains, and the game was much less abundant, while the natives had mostly left the river for their wintering grounds. I succeeded, nevertheless, in exchanging my goods for furs and dried fish, and a small supply of dried venison: and returned, on the 15th of November, to Astoria, where the want of fresh provisions began to be severely felt, so that several of the men were attacked with scurvy.

Messrs. Halsey and Wallace having been sent on the 23d, with fourteen men, to establish a trading post on the Willamet, and Mr. M'Dougal being confined to his room by sickness, Mr. Clapp and I were left with the entire charge of the post at Astoria, and were each other's only resource for society. Happily Mr. Clapp was a man of amiable character, of a gay, lively humor, and agreeable conversation. In the intervals of our daily duties, we amused ourselves with music and reading; having some instruments and a choice library. Otherwise we should have passed our time in a state of insufferable ennui, at this rainy season, in the midst of the deep mud which surrounded us, and which interdicted the pleasure of a promenade outside the buildings.

CHAPTER XIII.

Uneasiness respecting the "Beaver."—News of the Declaration of War between Great Britain and the United States.—Consequences of that Intelligence.—Different Occurrences.—Arrival of two Canoes of the Northwest Company.—Preparations for abandoning the Country.—Postponement of Departure.—Arrangement with Mr. J. G. M'Tavish.

The months of October, November, and December passed away without any news of the "Beaver," and we began to fear that there had happened to her, as to the Tonquin, some disastrous accident. It will be seen, in the following chapter, why this vessel did not return to Astoria in the autumn of 1812.

On the 15th of January, Mr. M'Kenzie arrived from the interior, having abandoned his trading establishment, after securing his stock of goods in a *cache*. Before his departure he had paid a visit to Mr. Clark on the Spokan, and while there had learned the news, which he came to announce to us, that hostilities had actually commenced between Great Britain and the United States. The news had been brought by some gentlemen of the Northwest Company, who handed to them a copy of the Proclamation of the President to that effect.

When we learned this news, all of us at Asto ria who were British subjects and Canadians, wished ourselves in Canada; but we could not entertain even the thought of transporting ourselves thither, at least immediately: we were separated from our country by an immense space, and the difficulties of the journey at this season were insuperable: besides, Mr. Astor's interests had to be consulted first. We held, therefore, a sort of council of war, to which the clerks of the factory were invited *pro formâ*, as they had no voice in the deliberations. Having maturely weighed our situation; after having seriously considered that being almost to a man British subjects, we were trading, notwithstanding, under the American flag: and foreseeing the improbability, or rather, to cut the matter short, the impossibility that Mr. Astor could send us further supplies or reinforcements while the war lasted, as most of the ports of the United States would inevitably be blockaded by the British; we concluded to abandon the establishment in the ensuing spring, or at latest, in the beginning of the summer. We did not communicate these resolutions to the men, lest they should in consequence abandon their labor: but we discontinued, from that moment, our trade with the natives, except for provisions; as well because we had no longer a large stock of goods on hand, as for the reason that we had already more furs than we could carry away overland.

So long as we expected the return of the vessel, we had served out to the people a regular supply of bread: we found ourselves in consequence, very short of provisions, on the arrival of Mr. M'Kenzie and his men. This augmentation in the number of mouths to be fed compelled us to reduce the ration of each man to four ounces of flour and half a pound of dried fish *per diem:*

and even to send a portion of the hands to pass the rest of the winter with Messrs. Wallace and Halsey on the Willamet, where game was plenty.

Meanwhile, the sturgeon having begun to enter the river, I left, on the 13th of February, to fish for them; and on the 15th sent the first boat-load to the establishment; which proved a very timely succor to the men, who for several days had broken off work from want of sufficient food. I formed a camp near Oak Point, whence I continued to despatch canoe after canoe of fine fresh fish to Astoria, and Mr. M'Dougal sent to me thither all the men who were sick of scurvy, for the re-establishment of their health.

On the 20th of March, Messrs. Reed and Seton, who had led a part of our men to the post on the Willamet, to subsist them, returned to Astoria, with a supply of dried venison. These gentlemen spoke to us in glowing terms of the country of the Willamet as charming, and abounding in beaver, elk, and deer; and informed us that Messrs. Wallace and Halsey had constructed a dwelling and trading house, on a great prairie, about one hundred and fifty miles from the confluence of that river with the Columbia. Mr. M'Kenzie and his party quitted us again on the 31st, to make known the resolutions recently adopted at Astoria, to the gentlemen who were wintering in the interior.

On the 11th of April two birch-bark canoes, bearing the British flag, arrived at the factory. They were commanded by Messrs. J. G. M'Tavish and Joseph Laroque, and manned by nineteen Canadian *voyageurs*. They landed on a point of land under the guns of the fort, and formed their camp. We invited these gentlemen to our quarters and learned from them the object of their visit. They had come to await the arrival of the ship *Isaac Todd*, despatched from Canada by the Northwest Company, in October, 1811, with furs, and from England in March, 1812, with a cargo of suitable merchandise for the Indian trade. They had orders to wait at the mouth of the Columbia till the month of July, and then to return, if the vessel did not make her appearance by that time. They also informed us that the natives near Lewis river had shown them fowling-pieces, gun-flints, lead, and powder; and that they had communicated this news to Mr. M'Kenzie, presuming that the Indians had discovered and plundered his *cache;* which turned out afterward to be the case.

The month of May was occupied in preparations for our departure from the Columbia. On the 25th, Messrs. Wallace and Halsey returned from their winter quarters with seventeen packs of furs, and thirty-two bales of dried venison. The last article was received with a great deal of pleasure, as it would infallibly be needed for the journey we were about to undertake. Messrs. Clarke, D. Stuart and M'Kenzie also arrived, in the beginning of June, with one hundred and forty packs of furs, the fruit of two years' trade at the post on the *Okenakan*, and one year on the *Spokan.**

The wintering partners (that is to say, Messrs. Clarke and David Stuart) dissenting from the

* The profits of the last establishment were slender; because the people engaged at it were obliged to subsist on horse-flesh, and they ate ninety horses during the winter.

proposal to abandon the country as soon as we intended, the thing being (as they observed) impracticable, from the want of provisions for the journey and horses to transport the goods, the project was deferred, as to its execution, till the following April. So these gentlemen, having taken a new lot of merchandise, set out again for their trading posts on the 7th of July. But Mr. M'Kenzie, whose goods had been pillaged by the natives (it will be remembered), remained at Astoria, and was occupied with the care of collecting as great a quantity as possible of dried salmon from the Indians. He made seven or eight voyages up the river for that purpose, while we at the Fort were busy in baling the beaver-skins and other furs, in suitable packs for horses to carry. Mr. Reed, in the meantime, was sent on to the mountain-passes where Mr. Miller had been left with the trappers, to winter there, and to procure as many horses as he could from the natives for our use in the contemplated journey. He was furnished for this expedition with three Canadians, and a half-breed hunter named *Daion*, the latter accompanied by his wife and two children. This man came from the lower Missouri with Mr. Hunt in 1811–'12.

Our object being to provide ourselves, before quitting the country, with the food and horses necessary for the journey; in order to avoid all opposition on the part of the Northwest Company, we entered into an arrangement with Mr. M'Tavish. This gentleman having represented to us that he was destitute of the necessary goods to procure wherewith to subsist his party on their way homeward, we supplied him from our warehouse, payment to be made us in the ensuing spring, either in furs or in bills of exchange on their house in Canada.

CHAPTER XIV.

Arrival of the Ship "Albatross."—Reasons for the Non-Appearance of the Beaver at Astoria.—Fruitless Attempt of Captain Smith on a Former Occasion.—Astonishment and Regret of Mr. Hunt at the Resolution of the Partners.—His Departure.—Narrative of the Destruction of the Tonquin.—Causes of that Disaster.—Reflections.

On the 4th of August, contrary to all expectation, we saw a sail at the mouth of the river. One of our gentlemen immediately got into the barge, to ascertain her nationality and object: but before he had fairly crossed the river, we saw her pass the bar and direct her course toward Astoria, as if she were commanded by a captain to whom the intricacies of the channel were familiar. I had stayed at the Fort with Mr. Clapp and four men. As soon as we had recognised the American flag, not doubting any longer that it was a ship destined for the factory, we saluted her with three guns. She came to anchor over against the fort, but on the opposite side of the river, and returned our salute. In a short time after, we saw, or rather we heard, the oars of a boat (for it was already night) that came toward us. We expected her approach with impatience, to know who the stranger was, and what news she brought us. Soon we were relieved from our uncertainty by the appearance of Mr. Hunt, who informed us that the ship was called the *Albatross* and was commanded by Captain *Smith*.

It will be remembered that Mr. Hunt had sailed from Astoria on board the "Beaver," on the 4th of August of the preceding year, and should have returned with that vessel, in the month of October of the same year. We testified to him our surprise that he had not returned at the time appointed, and expressed the fears which we had entertained in regard to his fate, as well as that of the Beaver itself: and in reply he explained to us the reasons why neither he nor Captain Sowles had been able to fulfil the promise which they had made us.

After having got clear of the river Columbia, they had scudded to the north, and had repaired to the Russian post of Chitka, where they had exchanged a part of their goods for furs. They had made with the governor of that establishment, Barnoff by name, arrangements to supply him regularly with all the goods of which he had need, and to send him every year a vessel for that purpose, as well as for the transportation of his surplus furs to the East Indies. They had then advanced still further to the north, to the coast of *Kamskatka;* and being there informed that some Kodiak hunters had been left on some adjacent isles, called the islands of St. Peter and St. Paul, and that these hunters had not been visited for three years, they determined to go thither, and having reached those isles, they opened a brisk trade, and secured no less than eighty thousand skins of the South-sea seal. These operations had consumed a great deal of time; the season was already far advanced; ice was forming around them, and it was not without having incurred considerable dangers that they succeeded in making their way out of those latitudes. Having extricated themselves from the frozen seas of the north, but in a shattered condition, they deemed it more prudent to run for the Sandwich isles, where they arrived after enduring a succession of severe gales. Here Mr. Hunt disembarked, with the men who had accompanied him, and who did not form a part of the ship's crew; and the vessel, after undergoing the necessary repairs, set sail for Canton.

Mr. Hunt had then passed nearly six months at the Sandwich islands, expecting the annual ship from New York, and never imagining that war had been declared. But at last, weary of waiting so long to no purpose, he had bought a small schooner of one of the chiefs of the isle of Wahoo, and was engaged in getting her ready to sail for the mouth of the Columbia, when four sails hove in sight, and presently came to anchor in *Ohetity bay*. He immediately went on board of one of them, and learned that they came from the Indies, whence they had sailed precipitately, to avoid the English cruisers. He also learned from the captain of the vessel he boarded, that the Beaver had arrived in Canton some days before the news of the declaration of war. This Captain Smith, moreover, had on board some cases of nankeens and other goods shipped by Mr. Astor's agent at Canton for us. Mr. Hunt then chartered the Albatross to take him with his people and the goods to the Columbia. That gentleman had not been idle during the time that he sojourned at Wahoo: he brought us 35 barrels of salt pork or beef, nine tierces of rice, a great quantity of dried *Taro*, and a good supply of salt.

As I knew the channel of the river, I went on board the Albatross, and piloted her to the old anchorage of the Tonquin, under the guns of the Fort, in order to facilitate the landing of the goods.

Captain Smith informed us that in 1810, a year before the founding of our establishment, he had entered the river in the same vessel, and ascended it in boats as far as Oak Point; and that he had attempted to form an establishment there; but the spot which he chose for building, and on which he had even commenced fencing for a garden, being overflowed in the summer freshet, he had been forced to abandon his project and re-embark. We had seen, in fact, at Oak Point, some traces of this projected establishment. The bold manner in which this captain had entered the river was now accounted for.

Captain Smith had chartered his vessel to a Frenchman named *Demestre*, who was then a passenger on board of her, to go and take a cargo of sandal wood at the *Marquesas*, where that gentleman had left some men to collect it, the year before. He could not, therefore, comply with the request we made him, to remain during the summer with us, in order to transport our goods and people, as soon as they could be got together, to the Sandwich islands.

Mr. Hunt was surprised beyond measure, when we informed him of the resolution we had taken of abandoning the country: he blamed us severely for having acted with so much precipitation, pointing out that the success of the late coasting voyage, and the arrangements we had made with the Russians, promised a most advantageous trade, which it was a thousand pities to sacrifice, and lose the fruits of the hardships he had endured and the dangers he had braved, at one fell swoop, by this rash measure. Nevertheless, seeing the partners were determined to abide by their first resolution, and not being able, by himself alone, to fulfil his engagements to Governor Barnoff, he consented to embark once more, in order to seek a vessel to transport our heavy goods, and such of us as wished to return by sea. He sailed, in fact, on the Albatross, at the end of the month. My friend Clapp embarked with him: they were, in the first instance, to run down the coast of California, in the hope of meeting there some of the American vessels which frequently visit that coast to obtain provisions from the Spaniards.

Some days after the departure of Mr. Hunt, the old one-eyed chief Comcomly came to tell us that an Indian of *Gray's Harbor*, who had sailed on the Tonquin in 1811, and who was the only soul that had escaped the massacre of the crew of that unfortunate vessel, had returned to his tribe. As the distance from the River Columbia to Gray's Harbor was not great, we sent for this native. At first he made considerable difficulty about following our people, but was finally persuaded. He arrived at Astoria, and related to us the circumstances of that sad catastrophe, nearly as follows:*

"After I had embarked on the Tonquin," said he, "that vessel sailed for *Nootka*.† Having arrived opposite a large village called *Newity*, we dropped anchor. The natives having invited Mr. M'Kay to land, he did so, and was received in the most cordial manner: they even kept him several days at their village, and made him lie,

* It being understood, of course, that I render into civilized expressions the language of this barbarian, and represent by words and phrases what he could only convey by gestures or by signs. [The *naïveté* of these notes, and of the narrative in these passages, is amusing.—Ed.]

† A great village or encampment of Indians, among whom the Spaniards had sent missionaries under the conduct of Signor Quadra; but whence the latter were chased by Captain Vancouver, in 1792, as mentioned in the Introduction.

every night, on a couch of sea-otter skins. Meanwhile the captain was engaged in trading with such of the natives as resorted to his ship: but having had a difficulty with one of the principal chiefs in regard to the price of certain goods, he ended by putting the latter out of the ship, and in the act of so repelling him, struck him on the face with the roll of furs which he had brought to trade. This act was regarded by that chief and his followers as the most grievous insult, and they resolved to take vengeance for it. To arrive more surely at their purpose, they dissembled their resentment, and came, as usual, on board the ship. One day, very early in the morning, a large pirogue, containing about a score of natives, came alongside: every man had in his hand a packet of furs, and held it over his head as a sign that they came to trade. The watch let them come on deck. A little after, arrived a second pirogue, carrying about as many men as the other. The sailors believed that these also came to exchange their furs, and allowed them to mount the ship's side like the first. Very soon, the pirogues thus succeeding one another, the crew saw themselves surrounded by a multitude of savages, who came upon the deck from all sides. Becoming alarmed at the appearance of things, they went to apprize the captain and Mr. M'Kay, who hastened to the poop. I was with them," said the narrator, "and fearing, from the great multitude of Indians whom I saw already on the deck, and from the movements of those on shore, who were hurrying to embark in their canoes, to approach the vessel, and from the women being left in charge of the canoes of those who had arrived, that some evil design was on foot, I communicated my suspicions to Mr. M'Kay, who himself spoke to the captain. The latter affected an air of security, and said that with the firearms on board, there was no reason to fear even a greater number of Indians. Meanwhile these gentlemen had come on deck unarmed, without even their sidearms. The trade, nevertheless, did not advance; the Indians offered less than was asked, and pressing with their furs close to the captain, Mr. M'Kay, and

Mr. Lewis, repeated the word *Makoke! Makoke!* "Trade! Trade!" I urged the gentlemen to put to sea, and the captain, at last, seeing the number of Indians increase every moment, allowed himself to be persuaded: he ordered a part of the crew to raise the anchor, and the rest to go aloft and unfurl the sails. At the same time he warned the natives to withdraw, as the ship was going to sea. A fresh breeze was then springing up, and in a few moments more their prey would have escaped them; but immediately on receiving this notice, by a preconcerted signal, the Indians, with a terrific yell, drew forth the knives and war-bludgeons they had concealed in their bundles of furs, and rushed upon the crew of the ship. Mr. Lewis was struck, and fell over a bale of blankets. Mr. M'Kay, however, was the first victim whom they sacrificed to their fury. Two savages, whom, from the crown of the poop, where I was seated, I had seen follow this gentleman step by step, now cast themselves upon him, and having given him a blow on the head with a *potumagan* (a kind of sabre which is described a little below), felled him to the deck, then took him up and flung him into the sea, where the women left in charge of the canoes, quickly finished him with their paddles. Another set flung themselves upon the captain, who defended himself for a long time with his pocket-knife, but, overpowered by numbers, perished also under the blows of these murderers. I next saw (and that was the last occurrence of which I was witness before quitting the ship) the sailors who were aloft, slip down by the rigging, and get below through the steerage hatchway. They were five, I think, in number, and one of them, in descending, received a knife-stab in the back. I then jumped overboard, to escape a similar fate to that of the captain and Mr. M'Kay: the women in the canoes, to whom I surrendered myself as a slave, took me in, and bade me hide myself under some mats which were in the pirogues; which I did. Soon after, I heard the discharge of firearms, immediately upon which the Indians fled from the vessel, and pulled for the shore as fast as possible, nor did they venture to go alongside the ship again the whole of that day. The next day, having seen four men lower a boat, and pull away from the ship, they sent some pirogues in chase: but whether those men were overtaken and murdered, or gained the open sea and perished there, I never could learn. Nothing more was seen stirring on board the Tonquin; the natives pulled cautiously around her, and some of the more daring went on board; at last, the savages, finding themselves absolute masters of the ship, rushed on board in a crowd to pillage her. But very soon, when there were about four or five hundred either huddled together on deck, or clinging to the sides, all eager for plunder, the ship blew up with a horrible noise. "I was on the shore," said the Indian, "when the explosion took place, saw the great volume of smoke burst forth in the spot where the ship had been, and high in the air above, arms, legs, heads and bodies, flying in every direction. The tribe acknowledged a loss of over two hundred of their people on that occasion. As for me I remained their prisoner, and have been their slave for two years. It is but now that I have been ransomed by my friends. I have told you the truth, and hope you will acquit me of having in any way participated in that bloody affair."

Our Indian having finished his discourse, we made him presents proportioned to the melancholy satisfaction he had given us in communicating the true history of the sad fate of our former companions, and to the trouble he had taken in coming to us; so that he returned apparently well satisfied with our liberality.

According to the narrative of this Indian, Captain Thorn, by his abrupt manner and passionate temper, was the primary cause of his own death and that of all on board his vessel. What appears certain at least, is, that he was guilty of unpardonable negligence and imprudence, in not causing the boarding netting to be rigged, as is the custom of all the navigators who frequent this coast, and in suffering (contrary to his instructions) too great a number of Indians to come on board at once.*

* It is equally evident that even at the time when Captain Thorn was first notified of the dangerous crowd and threatening

Captain Smith, of the Albatross, who had seen the wreck of the Tonquin, in mentioning to us its sad fate, attributed the cause of the disaster to the rash conduct of a Captain Ayres, of Boston. That navigator had taken off, as I have mentioned already, ten or a dozen natives of New-itty, as hunters, with a promise of bringing them back to their country, which promise he inhumanly broke by leaving them on some desert islands in Sir Francis Drake's Bay. The countrymen of these unfortunates, indignant at the conduct of the American captain, had sworn to avenge themselves on the first white men who appeared among them. Chance willed it that our vessel was the first to enter that bay, and the natives but too well executed on our people their project of vengeance.

Whatever may have been the first and principal cause of this misfortune (for doubtless it is

appearance of the natives, a display of firearms would have sufficed to prevent an outbreak. Had he come on deck with Mr. M'Kay and Mr. Lewis, each armed with a musket, and a couple of pistols at the belt, it is plain from the timidity the savages afterward displayed, that he might have cleared the ship, probably without shedding a drop of blood.—ED.

necessary to suppose more than one), seventeen white men and twelve Sandwich-Islanders, were massacred: not one escaped from the butchery, to bring us the news of it, but the Indian of *Gray's Harbor*. The massacre of our people was avenged, it is true, by the destruction of ten times the number of their murderers; but this circumstance, which could perhaps gladden the heart of a savage, was a feeble consolation (if it was any) for civilized men. The death of Mr. Alexander M'Kay was an irreparable loss to the Company, which would probably have been dissolved by the remaining partners, but for the arrival of the energetic Mr. Hunt. Interesting as was the recital of the Indian of Gray's Harbor throughout, when he came to the unhappy end of that estimable man, marks of regret were visibly painted on the countenances of all who listened.

At the beginning of September, Mr. M'Kenzie set off, with Messrs. Wallace and Seton, to carry a supply of goods to the gentlemen wintering in the interior, as well as to inform them of the arrangements concluded with Mr. Hunt, and to enjoin them to send down all their furs, and all the Sandwich-Islanders, that the former might be shipped for America, and the latter sent back to their country.

NOTE.

It will never be known how or by whom the *Tonquin* was blown up. Some pretend to say that it was the work of James Lewis, but that is impossible, for it appears from the narrative of the Indian that he was one of the first persons murdered. It will be recollected that five men got between decks from aloft, during the affray, and four only were seen to quit the ship afterward in the boat. The presumption was that the mis sing man must have done it, and in further conversation with the Gray's Harbor Indian, he inclined to that opinion, and even affirmed that the individual was the ship's armorer, *Weeks.* It might also have been accidental. There was a large quantity of powder in the run immediately under the cabin, and it is not impossible that while the Indians were intent on plunder, in opening some of the kegs they may have set fire to the contents. Or again, the men, before quitting the ship, may have lighted a slow train, which is the most likely supposition of all.

CHAPTER XV.

Arrival of a Number of Canoes of the Northwest Company.—Sale of the Establishment at Astoria to that Company.—Canadian News.—Arrival of the British Sloop-of-War "Racooon."—Accident on Board that Vessel.—The Captain takes Formal Possession of Astoria.—Surprise and Discontent of the Officers and Crew.—Departure of the "Raccoon."

A FEW days after Mr. M'Kenzie left us, we were greatly surprised by the appearance of two canoes bearing the British flag, with a third between them, carrying the flag of the United States, all rounding Tongue Point. It was no other than Mr. M'Kenzie himself, returning with Messrs. J. G. M'Tavish and Angus Bethune, of the Northwest Company. He had met these gentlemen near the first rapids, and had determined to return with them to the establishment, in consequence of information which they gave him. Those gentlemen were in *light* canoes

(i. e., without any lading), and formed the vanguard to a flotilla of eight, loaded with furs, under the conduct of Messrs. John Stuart and M'Millan.

Mr. M'Tavish came to our quarters at the factory, and showed Mr. M'Dougal a letter which had been addressed to the latter by Mr. Angus Shaw, his uncle, and one of the partners of the Northwest Company. Mr. Shaw informed his nephew that the ship *Isaac Todd* had sailed from London, with letters of *marque*, in the month of March, in company with the frigate *Phœbe*, having orders from the government to seize our establishment, which had been represented to the lords of the admiralty as an important colony founded by the American government. The eight canoes left behind, came up meanwhile, and uniting themselves to the others, they formed a camp of about seventy-five men, at the bottom of a little bay or cove, near our factory. As they were destitute of provisions, we supplied them; but Messrs. M'Dougal and M'Kenzie affecting to dread a surprise from this British force under our guns, we kept strictly on our guard; for we were inferior in point of numbers, although our position was exceedingly advantageous.

As the season advanced, and their ship did not arrive, our new neighbors found themselves in a very disagreeable situation, without food, or merchandise wherewith to procure it from the natives; viewed by the latter with a distrustful and hostile eye, as being our enemies and therefore exposed to attack and plunder on their part with impunity; supplied with good hunters, indeed, but wanting ammunition to render their skill available. Weary, at length, of applying to us incessantly for food (which we furnished them with a sparing hand), unable either to retrace their steps through the wilderness or to remain in their present position, they came to the conclusion of proposing to buy of us the whole establishment.

Placed, as we were, in the situation of expecting, day by day, the arrival of an English ship-of-war to seize upon all we possessed, we listened to their propositions. Several meetings and discussions took place; the negotiations were protracted by the hope of one party that the long-expected armed force would arrive, to render the purchase unnecessary, and were urged forward by the other in order to conclude the affair before that occurrence should intervene; at length the price of the goods and furs in the factory was agreed upon, and the bargain was signed by both parties on the 23d of October. The gentlemen of the Northwest Company took possession of Astoria, agreeing to pay the servants of the Pacific Fur Company (the name which had been chosen by Mr. Astor), the arrears of their wages, to be deducted from the price of the goods which we delivered, to supply them with provisions, and give a free passage to those who wished to return to Canada over land. The American colors were hauled down from the factory, and the British run up, to the no small chagrin and mortification of those who were American citizens.

It was thus, that after having passed the seas, and suffered all sorts of fatigues and privations, I lost in a moment all my hopes of fortune. I could not help remarking that we had no right to expect such treatment on the part of the British government, after the assurances we had received from Mr. Jackson, his majesty's *chargé d'affaires* previously to our departure from New York. But as I have just intimated, the agents of the Northwest Company had exaggerated the importance of the factory in the eyes of the British ministry; for if the latter had known what it really was—a mere trading-post—and that nothing but the rivalry of the fur-traders of the Northwest Company was interested in its destruction, they would never have taken umbrage at it, or at least would never have sent a maritime expedition to destroy it. The sequel will show that I was not mistaken in this opinion.

The greater part of the servants of the Pacific Fur Company entered the service of the Company of the Northwest: the rest preferred to return to their country, and I was of the number of these last. Nevertheless, Mr. M'Tavish, after many ineffectual attempts to persuade me to remain with them, having intimated that the establishment could not dispense with my services, as I was the only person who could assist them in their trade, especially for provisions, of which they would soon be in the greatest need, I agreed with them (without however relinquishing my previous engagement with Mr. Astor's agents) for five months, that is to say, till the departure of the expedition which was to ascend the Columbia in the spring, and reach Canada by way of the Rocky Mountains and the rivers of the interior. Messrs. John Stuart and M'Kenzie set off about the end of this month, for the interior, in order that the latter might make over to the former the posts established on the Spokan and Okenakan.

On the 15th of November, Messrs. Alexander Stuart and Alexander Henry, both partners of the N. W. Company, arrived at the factory, in a couple of bark canoes manned by sixteen *voyageurs.* They had set out from *Fort William*, on Lake Superior, in the month of July. They brought us Canadian papers, by which we learned that the British arms so far had been in the ascendant. They confirmed also the news that an English frigate was coming to take possession of our quondam establishment; they were even surprised not to see the *Isaac Todd* lying in the road.

On the morning of the 30th, we saw a large vessel standing in under *Cape Disappointment* (which proved in this instance to deserve its name); and soon after that vessel came to anchor in *Baker's bay*. Not knowing whether it was a friendly or a hostile sail, we thought it prudent to send on board Mr. M'Dougal in a canoe, manned by such of the men as had been previously in the service of the Pacific Fur Company, with injunctions to declare themselves Americans, if the vessel was American, and Englishmen in the contrary case. While this party was on its way, Mr. M'Tavish caused all the furs which were marked with the initials of the N. W. Company to be placed on board the two barges at the Fort, and sent them up the river above Tongue Point, where they were to wait for a concerted signal, that was to inform them whether the new-comers were friends or foes. Toward midnight, Mr. Halsey, who had accompanied Mr. M'Dougal to the vessel, returned to the Fort, and announced to us that she was the British sloop-of-war *Raccoon*, of 26 guns, commanded by Captain Black, with a complement of 120 men, fore and aft. Mr. John M'Donald, a partner of the N. W. Company, was a passenger on the Raccoon, with five *voyageurs*, destined for the Company's service. He had left England in the frigate *Phœbe*, which had sailed in company with the *Isaac Todd* as far as Rio Janeiro; but there falling in with the British squadron, the admiral changed the destination of the frigate, despatching the sloops-of-war *Raccoon* and *Cherub* to convoy the Isaac Todd, and sent the Phœbe to search for the American commodore Porter, who was then on the Pacific, capturing all the British whalers and other trading vessels he met with. These four vessels then sailed in company as far as Cape Horn, where they parted, after agreeing on the island of *Juan Fernandez* as a *rendezvous*. The three ships-of-war met, in fact, at that island; but after having a long time waited in vain for the *Isaac Todd*, Commodore Hillier (Hillyer?) who commanded this little squadron, hearing of the injury inflicted by Commodore Porter, on the British commerce, and especially on the whalers who frequent these seas, resolved to go in quest of him in order to give him combat; and retaining the *Cherub* to assist him, detailed the Raccoon to go and destroy the American establishment on the River Columbia, being assured by Mr. M'Donald that a single sloop-of-war would be sufficient for that service.

Mr. M'Donald had consequently embarked, with his people, on board the Raccoon. This gentleman informed us that they had experienced frightful weather in doubling the Cape, and that he entertained serious apprehensions for the safety of the Isaac Todd, but that if she was safe, we might expect her to arrive in the river in two or three weeks. The signal gun agreed upon, having been fired, for the return of the barges, Mr. M'Tavish came back to the Fort with the furs, and was overjoyed to learn the arrival of Mr. M'Donald.

On the 1st of December the Raccoon's gig came up to the fort, bringing Mr. M'Donald (surnamed *Bras Croche*, or crooked arm), and the first lieutenant, Mr. Sheriff. Both these gentlemen were convalescent from the effects of an accident which had happened to them in the passage between Juan Fernandez and the mouth of the Columbia. The captain wishing to clean the guns, ordered them to be scaled, that is, fired off: during this exercise one of the guns hung fire; the sparks fell into a cartridge tub, and setting fire to the combustibles, communicated also to some priming horns suspended above; an explosion followed, which reached some twenty persons; eight were killed on the spot, the rest were severely burnt; Messrs. M'Donald and Sheriff had suffered a great deal; it was with difficulty that their clothes had been removed; and when the lieutenant came ashore, he had not recovered the use of his hands. Among the killed was an American named *Flatt*, who was in the service of the Northwest Company and whose loss these gentlemen appeared exceedingly to regret.

As there were goods destined for the Company on board the Raccoon, the schooner *Dolly* was sent to Baker's bay to bring them up: but the weather was so bad, and the wind so violent, that she did not return till the 12th, bringing up, together with the goods, Captain Black, a lieutenant of marines, four soldiers and as many sailors. We entertained our guests as splendidly as it lay in our power to do. After dinner, the captain caused firearms to be given to the servants of the Company, and we all marched under arms to the square or platform, where a flag-staff had been erected. There the captain took a British Union Jack, which he had brought on shore for the occasion, and caused it to be run up to the top of the staff; then, taking a bottle of Madeira wine, he broke it on the flag-staff, declaring in a loud voice, that he took possession of the establishment and of the country in the name of His Britannic Majesty; and changed the name of Astoria to *Fort George*. Some few Indian chiefs had been got together to witness this ceremony, and I explained to them in their own language what it signified. Three rounds of artillery and musketry were fired, and the health of the king was drunk by the parties interested, according to the usage on like occasions.

The sloop being detained by contrary winds, the captain caused an exact survey to be made of the entrance of the river, as well as of the navigable channel between Baker's bay and Fort George. The officers visited the fort, turn about, and seemed to me in general very much dissatisfied with their fool's errand, as they called it: they had expected to find a number of American vessels loaded with rich furs, and had calculated in advance their share in the booty of Astoria. They had not met a vessel, and their astonishment was at its height when they saw that our establishment had been transferred to the Northwest Company, and was under the British flag. It will suffice to quote a single expression of Captain Black's, in order to show

how much they were deceived in their expectations. The Captain landed after dark; when we showed him the next morning the palisades and log bastions of the factory, he inquired if there was not another fort; on being assured that there was no other, he cried out, with an air of the greatest astonishment:—"What! is this the fort which was represented to me as so formidable! Good God! I could batter it down in two hours with a four-pounder!"

There were on board the Raccoon two young men from Canada, who had been impressed at Quebec, when that vessel was there some years before her voyage to the Columbia: one of them was named *Parent*, a blacksmith, and was of Quebec: the other was from Upper Canada, and was named M'Donald. These young persons signified to us that they would be glad to remain at Fort George: and as there was among our men some who would gladly have shipped, we proposed to the captain an exchange, but he would not consent to it. John Little, a boatbuilder from New York, who had been on the sick list a long time, was sent on board and placed under the care of the sloop's surgeon, Mr. O'Brien; the captain engaging to land him at the Sandwich Islands. P. D. Jeremie also shipped himself as under clerk. The vessel hoisted sail, and got out of the river, on the 31st of December.

From the account given in this chapter the reader will see with what facility the establishment of the Pacific Fur Company could have escaped capture by the British force. It was only necessary to get rid of the land party of the Northwest Company—who were completely in our power—then remove our effects up the river upon some small stream, and await the result. The sloop-of-war arrived, it is true; but as, in the case I suppose, she would have found nothing, she would have left, after setting fire to our deserted houses. None of their boats would have dared follow us, even if the Indians had betrayed to them our lurking-place. Those at the head of affairs had their own fortunes to seek, and thought it more for their interest, doubtless, to act as they did, but that will not clear them in the eyes of the world, and the charge of treason to Mr. Astor's interests will always be attached to their characters.

CHAPTER XVI.

Expeditions to the Interior.—Return of Messrs. John Stuart and D. M'Kenzie.—Theft committed by the Natives.—War Party against the Thieves.

On the 3d of January, 1814, two canoes laden with merchandise for the interior, were despatched under the command of Mr. Alexander Stuart and Mr. James Keith, with fifteen men under them. Two of the latter were charged with letters for the posts (of the Northwest Company) east of the mountains, containing instructions to the persons in superintendence there, to have in readiness canoes and the requisite provisions for a large party intending to go east the ensuing spring. I took this opportunity of advising my friends in Canada of my intention to return home that season. It was the third attempt I had made to send news of my existence to my relatives and friends: the first two had miscarried and this was doomed to meet the same fate.

Messrs. J. Stuart and M'Kenzie, who (as was seen in a previous chapter) had been sent to notify the gentlemen in the interior of what had taken place at Astoria, and to transfer the wintering posts to the Northwest Company, returned to Fort George on the morning of the 6th. They stated that they had left Messrs. Clarke and D. Stuart behind, with the loaded canoes, and also that the party had been attacked by the natives above the falls.

As they were descending the river toward evening, between the first and second portages, they had espied a large number of Indians congregated at no great distance in the prairie; which gave them some uneasiness. In fact, some time after they had encamped, and when all the people (*tout le monde*) were asleep, except Mr. Stuart, who was on guard, these savages had stealthily approached the camp, and discharged some arrows, one of which had penetrated the coverlet of one of the men, who was lying near the baggage, and had pierced the cartilage of his ear; the pain made him utter a sharp cry, which alarmed the whole camp and threw it into an uproar. The natives perceiving it, fled to the woods, howling and yelling like so many demons. In the morning our people picked up eight arrows round the camp: they could yet hear the savages yell and whoop in the woods: but, notwithstanding, the party reached the lower end of the portage unmolested.

The audacity which these barbarians had displayed in attacking a party of from forty to forty-five persons, made us suppose that they would, much more probably, attack the party of Mr. Stuart, which was composed of but seventeen men. Consequently, I received orders to get ready forthwith a canoe and firearms, in order to proceed to their relief. The whole was ready in the short space of two hours, and I embarked immediately with a guide and eight men. Our instructions were to use all possible diligence to overtake Messrs. Stewart and Keith, and to convey them to the upper end of the last portage; or to return with the goods, if we met too much resistance on the part of the natives. We travelled, then, all that day, and all the night of the 6th, and on the 7th, till evening. Finding ourselves then at a little distance from the rapids, I came to a halt, to put the firearms in order, and let the men take some repose. About midnight I caused them to re-embark, and ordered the men to sing as they rowed, that the party whom we wished to overtake might hear us as we passed, if perchance they were encamped on some one of the islands of which the river is full in this part. In fact, we had hardly proceeded five or six miles, when we were hailed by some one apparently in the middle of the stream. We stopped rowing, and answered, and were soon joined by our people of the expedition, who were all descending the river in a canoe. They informed us that they had been attacked the evenning before, and that Mr. Stuart had been wounded. We turned about, and all proceeded in company toward the fort. In the morning, when we stopped to breakfast, Mr. Keith gave me the particulars of the affair of the day preceding.

Having arrived at the foot of the rapids, they commenced the portage on the south bank of the river, which is obstructed with boulders, over which it was necessary to pass the effects. After they had hauled over the two canoes, and a part of the goods, the natives approached in great numbers, trying to carry off something unobserved. Mr. Stuart was at the upper end of the portage (the portage being about six hundred yards in length), and Mr. Keith accompanied the loaded men. An Indian seized a bag containing articles of little value, and fled: Mr. Stuart, who saw the act, pursued the thief, and after some resistance on the latter's part, succeeded in making him relinquish his booty. Immediately he saw a number of Indians armed with bows and arrows, approaching him: one of them bent his bow and took aim; Mr. Stuart, on his part, levelled his gun at the Indian, warning the latter not to shoot, and at the same instant received an arrow, which pierced his left shoulder. He then drew the trigger; but as it had rained all day, the gun missed fire, and before he could re-prime, another arrow, better aimed than the first, struck him in the left side and penetrated between two of his ribs, in the region of the heart, and would have proved fatal, no doubt, but for a stone-pipe he had fortunately in his side-pocket, and which was broken by the arrow; at the same moment his gun was discharged, and the Indian fell dead. Several others then rushed forward to avenge the death of their compatriot; but two of the men came up with their loads and their gun (for these portages were made arms in hand), and seeing what was going forward, one of them threw his pack on the ground, fired on one of the Indians and brought him down. He got up again, however, and picked up his weapons, but the other man ran upon him, wrested from him his war-club, and despatched him by repeated blows on the head with it. The other savages, seeing the bulk of our people approaching the scene of combat, retired and crossed the river. In the meantime, Mr. Stuart extracted the arrows from his body, by the aid of one of the men: the blood flowed in abundance from the wounds, and he saw that it would be impossible for him to pursue his journey; he therefore gave orders for the canoes and goods to be carried back to the lower end of the portage. Presently they saw a great number of pirogues full of warriors coming from the opposite side of the river. Our people then considered that they could do nothing better than to get away as fast as possible; they contrived to transport over one canoe, on which they all embarked, abandoning the other and the goods, to the natives. While the barbarians were plundering these effects, more precious in their estimation than the apples of gold in the garden of the Hesperides, our party retired and got out of sight. The retreat was, notwithstanding, so precipitate, that they left behind an Indian from the Lake of the Two Mountains, who was in the service of the Company as a hunter. This Indian had persisted in concealing himself behind the rocks, meaning, he said, to kill some of those thieves, and did not return in time for the embarkation. Mr. Keith regretted this brave man's obstinacy, fearing, with good reason, that he would be discovered and murdered by the natives. We rowed all that day and night, and reached the factory on the 9th, at sunrise. Our first care, after having announced the misfortune of our people, was to dress the wounds of Mr. Stuart, which had been merely bound with a wretched piece of cotton cloth.

The goods which had been abandoned, were of consequence to the Company, inasmuch as they could not be replaced. It was dangerous, besides, to leave the natives in possession of some fifty guns and a considerable quantity of ammunition, which they might use against us.* The partners, therefore, decided to fit out an expedition immediately to chastise the robbers, or at least to endeavor to recover the goods. I went, by their order, to find the principal chiefs of the neighboring tribes, to explain to them what had

* However, some cases of guns and kegs of powder were thrown into the falls, before the party retreated.

taken place, and invite them to join us, to which they willingly consented. Then, having got ready six canoes, we re-embarked on the 10th, to the number of sixty-two men, all armed from head to foot, and provided with a small brass field-piece.

We soon reached the lower end of the first rapid: but the essential thing was wanting to our little force; it was without provisions; our first care then was to try to procure these. Having arrived opposite a village, we perceived on the bank about thirty armed savages, who seemed to await us firmly. As it was not our policy to seem bent on hostilities, we landed on the opposite bank, and I crossed the river with five or six men, to enter into parley with them, and try to obtain provisions. I immediately became aware that the village was abandoned, the women and children having fled to the woods, taking with them all the articles of food. The young men, however, offered us dogs, of which we purchased a score. Then we passed to a second village, where they were already informed of our coming. Here we bought forty-five dogs and a horse. With this stock we formed an encampment on an island called *Strawberry island.*

Seeing ourselves now provided with food for several days, we informed the natives touching the motives which had brought us, and announced to them that we were determined to put them all to death and burn their villages, if they did not bring back in two days the effects stolen on the 7th. A party was detached to the rapids, where the attack on Mr. Stuart had taken place. We found the villages all deserted. Crossing to the north bank, we found a few natives, of whom we made inquiries respecting the Nipissingue Indian, who had been left behind, but they assured us that they had seen nothing of him.*

* This Indian returned some time after to the factory, but in a pitiable condition. After the departure of the canoe, he had concealed himself behind a rock, and so passed the night. At day-break, fearing to be discovered, he gained the woods and directed his steps toward the fort, across a mountainous region. He arrived at length at the bank of a little stream, which he was at first unable to cross. Hunger, in the meantime, began to urge him; he might have appeased it with game, of which he saw plenty, but unfortunately he had lost the flint of his gun. At last, with a

Not having succeeded in recovering, above the rapids, any part of the lost goods, the inhabitants all protesting that it was not they, but the villages below, which had perpetrated the robbery, we descended the river again, and re-encamped on *Strawberry island.* As the intention of the partners was to intimidate the natives, without (if possible) shedding blood, we made a display of our numbers, and from time to time fired off our little field-piece, to let them see that we could reach them from one side of the river to the other. The Indian *Coalpo* and his wife, who had accompanied us, advised us to make prisoner one of the chiefs. We succeeded in this design, without incurring any danger. Having invited one of the natives to come and smoke with us, he came accordingly: a little after, came another; at last, one of the chiefs, and he one of the most considered among them, also came. Being notified secretly of his character

raft of sticks, he crossed the river, and arrived at a village, the inhabitants of which disarmed him, and made him prisoner. Our people hearing where he was, sent to seek him, and gave some blankets for his ransom.

by *Coalpo*, who was concealed in the tent, we seized him forthwith, tied him to a stake, and placed a guard over him with a naked sword, as if ready to cut his head off on the least attempt being made by his people for his liberation. The other Indians were then suffered to depart with the news for his tribe, that unless the goods were brought to us in twenty-four hours, their chief would be put to death. Our stratagem succeeded: soon after we heard wailing and lamentation in the village, and they presently brought us part of the guns, some brass kettles, and a variety of smaller articles, protesting that this was all their share of the plunder. Keeping our chief as a hostage, we passed to the other village, and succeeded in recovering the rest of the guns, and about a third of the other goods.

Although they had been the aggressors, yet as they had had two men killed and we had not lost any on our side, we thought it our duty to conform to the usage of the country, and abandon to them the remainder of the stolen effects, to cover, according to their expression, the bodies of their two slain compatriots. Besides, we began to find ourselves short of provisions, and it would not have been easy to get at our enemies to punish them, if they had taken refuge in the woods, according to their custom when they feel themselves the weaker party. So we released our prisoner, and gave him a flag, telling him that when he presented it unfurled, we should regard it as a sign of peace and friendship: but if, when we were passing the portage, any one of the natives should have the misfortune to come near the baggage, we would kill him on the spot. We re-embarked on the 19th, and on the 22d reached the fort, where we made a report of our martial expedition. We found Mr. Stuart very ill of his wounds, especially of the one in the side, which was so much swelled that we had every reason to think the arrow had been poisoned.

If we did not do the savages as much harm as we might have done, it was not from timidity but from humanity, and in order not to shed human blood uselessly. For after all, what good would it have done us to have slaughtered some of these barbarians, whose crime was not the effect of depravity and wickedness, but of an ardent and irresistible desire to ameliorate their condition? It must be allowed also that the interest, well-understood, of the partners of the Northwest Company, was opposed to too strongly marked acts of hostility on their part: it behooved them exceedingly not to make irreconciliable enemies of the populations neighboring on the portages of the Columbia, which they would so often be obliged to pass and repass in future. It is also probable that the other natives on the banks, as well as of the river as of the sea, would not have seen with indifference, their countrymen too signally or too rigorously punished by strangers; and that they would have made common cause with the former to resist the latter, and perhaps even to drive them from the country.

I must not omit to state that all the firearms surrendered by the Indians on this occasion, were found loaded with ball, and primed, with a little piece of cotton laid over the priming to keep the powder dry. This shows how soon they would acquire the use of guns, and how careful traders should be in intercourse with strange Indians, not to teach them their use.

CHAPTER XVII.

Description of Tongue Point.—A Trip to the *Willamet.*—Arrival of W. Hunt in the Brig Pedlar.—Narrative of the Loss of the Ship Lark.—Preparations for crossing the Continent.

THE new proprietors of our establishment, being dissatisfied with the site we had chosen, came to the determination to change it; after surveying both sides of the river, they found no better place than the head-land which we had named Tongue point. This point, or to speak more accurately, perhaps, this cape, extends about a quarter of a mile into the river, being connected with the main-land by a low, narrow neck, over which the Indians, in stormy weather, haul their canoes in passing up and down the river; and terminating in an almost perpendicular rock, of about 250 or 300 feet elevation. This bold summit was covered with a dense forest of pine trees; the ascent from the lower neck was gradual and easy; it abounded in springs of the finest water; on either side it had a cove to shelter the boats necessary for a trading establishment. This peninsula had truly the appearance of a huge tongue. Astoria had been built nearer the ocean, but the advantages offered by Tongue point more than compensated for its greater distance. Its soil, in the rainy season, could be drained with little or no trouble; it was a better position to guard against attacks on the part of the natives, and less exposed to that of civilized enemies by sea or land in time of war.

All the hands who had returned from the interior, added to those who were already at the Fort, consumed, in an incredibly short space of time the small stock of provisions which had been conveyed by the Pacific Fur Company to the Company of the Northwest. It became a matter of necessity, therefore, to seek some spot where a part, at least, could be sent to subsist. With these views I left the fort on the 7th February with a number of men, belonging to the old concern, and who had refused to enter the service of the new one, to proceed to the establishment on the *Willamet* river, under the charge of Mr. Alexander Henry, who had with him a number of first-rate hunters. Leaving the Columbia to ascend the *Willamet*, I found the banks on either side of that stream well wooded, but low and swampy, until I reached the first falls; having passed which, by making a portage, I commenced ascending a clear but moderately deep channel, against a swift current. The banks on either side were bordered with forest-trees, but behind that narrow belt, diversified with prairie, the landscape was magnificent; the hills were of moderate elevation, and rising in an amphitheatre. Deer and elk are found here in great abundance; and the post in charge of Mr. Henry had been established with a view of keeping constantly there a number of hunters to prepare dried venison for the use of the factory. On our arrival at the Columbia, considering the latitude, we had expected severe winter weather, such as is experienced in the same latitudes east; but we were soon undeceived; the mildness of the climate never permitted us to transport fresh provisions from the Willamet to Astoria. We had not a particle of salt; and the attempts we made to smoke or dry the venison proved abortive.

Having left the men under my charge with Mr. Henry, I took leave of that gentleman, and returned. At Oak point I found Messrs. Keith and Pillet encamped, to pass there the season of sturgeon-fishing. They informed me that I was to stay with them.

Accordingly I remained at Oak point the rest of the winter, occupied in trading with the Indians spread all along the river for some 30 or 40 miles above, in order to supply the factory with provisions. I used to take a boat with four or five men, visit every fishing station, trade for as much fish as would load the boat, and send her down to the fort. The surplus fish traded in the interval between the departure and return of the boat, was cut up, salted and barrelled for future use. The salt had been recently obtained from a quarter to be presently mentioned.

About the middle of March Messrs. Keith and Pillet both left me and returned to the fort. Being now alone, I began seriously to reflect on my position, and it was in this interval that I positively decided to return to Canada. I made inquiries of the men sent up with the boats for fish, concerning the preparations for departure, but whether they had been enjoined secrecy, or were unwilling to communicate, I could learn nothing of what was doing below.

At last I heard that on the 28th February a sail had appeared at the mouth of the river. The gentlemen of the N. W. Company at first flattered themselves that it was the vessel they had so long expected. They were soon undeceived by a letter from Mr. Hunt, which was brought to the fort by the Indians of *Baker's bay*. That gentleman had purchased at the Marquesas islands a brig called *The Pedlar:* it was on that vessel that he arrived, having for pilot Captain Northrop, formerly commander of the ship *Lark*. The latter vessel had been outfitted by Mr. Astor, and despatched from New York, in spite of the blockading squadron, with supplies for the *ci-devant* Pacific Fur Company; but unhappily she had been assailed by a furious tempest and capsized in lat. 16° N., and three or four hundred miles from the Sandwich Islands. The mate, who was sick, was drowned in the cabin, and four of the crew perished at the same time. The captain had the masts and rigging cut away, which caused the vessel to right again, though full of water. One of the hands dived down to the sail-maker's locker, and got out a small sail, which they attached to the bowsprit. He dived a second time, and brought up a box containing a dozen bottles of wine. For thirteen days they had no other sustenance but the flesh of a small shark, which they had the good fortune to take, and which they ate raw, and for drink, a gill of the wine each man *per diem*. At last the trade winds carried them upon the island of *Tahouraka*, where the vessel went to pieces on the reef. The islanders saved the crew, and seized all the goods which floated on the water. Mr. Hunt was then at *Wahoo*, and learned through some islanders from *Morotoi*, that some Americans had been wrecked on the isle of *Tahouraka*. He went immediately to take them off, and gave the pilotage of his own vessel to Captain Northrop.

It may be imagined what was the surprise of Mr. Hunt when he saw Astoria under the British flag, and passed into stranger hands. But the misfortune was beyond remedy, and he was obliged to content himself with taking on board all the Americans who were at the establishment, and who had not entered the service of the Company of the Northwest. Messrs. Halsey, Seton, and Farnham were among those who embarked. I shall have occasion to inform the reader of the part each of them played, and how they reached their homes.

When I heard that Mr. Hunt was in the river, and knowing that the overland expedition was to set out early in April, I raised camp at Oak point, and reached the fort on the 2d of that month. But the brig *Pedlar* had that very day got outside the river, after several fruitless attempts, in one of which she narrowly missed being lost on the bar.

I would gladly have gone in her, had I but arrived a day sooner. I found, however, all things prepared for the departure of the canoes, which was to take place on the 4th. I got ready the few articles I possessed, and in spite of the very advantageous offers of the gentlemen of the N. W. Company, and their reiterated persuasions, aided by the crafty M'Dougal, to induce me to remain, at least one year more, I persisted in my resolution to leave the country. The journey I was about to undertake was a long one: it would be accompanied with great fatigues and many privations, and even by some dangers; but I was used to privations and fatigues; I had braved dangers of more than one sort; and even had it been otherwise, the ardent desire of revisiting my country, my relatives, and my friends, the hope of finding myself, in a few months, in their midst, would have made me overlook every other consideration.

I am about, then, to quit the banks of the river Columbia, and conduct the reader through the mountain passes, over the plains, the forests, and the lakes of our continent: but I ought first to give him at least an idea of the manners and customs of the inhabitants, as well as of the principal productions of the country that I now quit, after a sojourn of three years. This is what I shall try to do in the following chapters.*

* Some of my readers would, no doubt, desire some scientific details on the botany and natural history of this country. That is, in fact, what they ought to expect from a man who had travelled for his pleasure, or to make discoveries: but the object of my travels was not of this description; my occupations had no relation with science; and, as I have said in my preface, I was not, and am not now, either a naturalist or a botanist.

CHAPTER XVIII.

Situation of the Columbia River.—Qualities of its Soil.—Climate, &c.—Vegetable and Animal Productions of the Country.

THE mouth of the Columbia river is situated in 46° 19′ north latitude, and 125° or 126° of longitude west of the meridian of Greenwich. The highest tides are very little over nine or ten feet, at its entrance, and are felt up stream for a distance of twenty-five or thirty leagues.

During the three years I spent there, the cold never was much below the freezing point; and I do not think the heat ever exceeded 76°. Westerly winds prevail from the early part of spring, and during a part of the summer; that wind generally springs up with the flood tide, and tempers the heat of the day. The northwest wind prevails during the latter part of summer and commencement of autumn. This last is succeeded by a southeast wind, which blows almost without intermission from the beginning of October to the end of December, or commencement of January. This interval is the rainy season, the most disagreeable of the year. Fogs (so thick that sometimes for days no object is discernible for five or six hundred yards from the beach), are also very prevalent.

The surface of the soil consists (in the valleys) of a layer of black vegetable mould, about five or six inches thick at most; under this layer is found another of gray and loose, but extremely cold earth; below which is a bed of coarse sand and gravel, and next to that pebble or hard rock. On the more elevated parts, the same black vegetable mould is found, but much thinner, and under it is the trap rock. We found along the seashore, south of Point Adams, a bank of earth white as chalk, which we used for white-washing our walls. The natives also brought us several specimens of blue, red and yellow earth or clay, which they said was to be found at a great distance south; and also a sort of shining earth, resembling lead ore.* We found no limestone, although we burnt several kilns, but never could get one ounce of lime.

We had brought with us from New York a variety of garden seeds, which were put in the ground in the month of May, 1811, on a rich piece of land laid out for the purpose on a sloping ground in front of our establishment. The garden had a fine appearance in the month of August; but although the plants were left in the ground until December, not one of them came to maturity, with the exception of the radishes, the turnips, and the potatoes. The turnips grew to a prodigious size; one of the largest we had the curiosity to weigh and measure; its circumference was thirty-three inches, its weight fifteen and a half pounds. The radishes were in full blossom in the month of December, and were left in the ground to perfect the seeds for the ensuing season, but they were all destroyed by the ground mice, who hid themselves under the stumps which

* Plumbago.

we had not rooted out, and infested our garden. With all the care we could bestow on them during the passage from New York, only twelve potatoes were saved, and even these so shrivelled up, that we despaired of raising any from the few sprouts that still gave signs of life. Nevertheless we raised one hundred and ninety potatoes the first season, and after sparing a few plants for our inland traders, we planted about fifty or sixty hills, which produced five bushels the second year; about two of these were planted, and gave us a welcome crop of fifty bushels in the year 1813.

It would result from these facts, that the soil on the banks of the river, as far as tide water, or for a distance of fifty or sixty miles, is very little adapted for agriculture; at all events, vegetation is very slow. It may be that the soil is not everywhere so cold as the spot we selected for our garden, and some other positions might have given a better reward for our labor: this supposition is rendered more than probable when we take into consideration the great difference in the indigenous vegetables of the country in different localities.

The forest trees most common at the mouth of the river and near our establishment, were cedar, hemlock, white and red spruce, and alder. There were a few dwarf white and gray ashes; and here and there a soft maple. The alder grows also to a very large size; I measured some of twelve to fifteen inches diameter; the wood was used by us in preference, to make charcoal for the blacksmith's forge. But the largest of all the trees that I saw in the country, was a white spruce: this tree, which had lost its top branches, and bore evident marks of having been struck by lightning, was a mere, straight trunk of about eighty to one hundred feet in height; its bark whitened by age, made it very conspicuous among the other trees with their brown bark and dark foliage, like a huge column of white marble. It stood on the slope of a hill immediately in the rear of our palisades. Seven of us placed ourselves round its trunk, and we could not embrace it by extending our arms and touching merely the tips of our fingers; we measured it afterward in a more regular manner, and found it forty-two feet in circumference. It kept the same size, or nearly the same, to the very top.

We had it in contemplation at one time to construct a circular staircase to its summit, and erect a platform thereon for an observatory, but more necessary and pressing demands on our time made us abandon the project.

A short distance above Astoria, the oak and ash are plentiful, but neither of these is of much value or beauty.

From the middle of June to the middle of October, we had abundance of wild fruit; first, strawberries, almost white, small but very sweet; then raspberries, both red and orange color. These grow on a bush sometimes twelve feet in height: they are not sweet, but of a large size.

The months of July and August furnish a small berry of an agreeable, slightly acid flavor; this berry grows on a slender bush of some eight to nine feet high, with small round leaves; they are in size like a wild cherry: some are blue, while others are of a cherry red: the last being smaller; they have no pits, or stones in them, but seeds, such as are to be seen in currants.

I noticed in the month of August another berry growing in bunches or grapes like the currant, on a bush very similar to the currant bush: the leaves of this shrub resemble those of the laurel: they are very thick and always green. The fruit is oblong, and disposed in two rows on the stem: the extremity of the berry is open, having a little speck or tuft like that of an apple. It is not of a particularly fine flavor, but it is wholesome, and one may eat a quantity of it, without inconvenience. The natives make great use of it; they prepare it for the winter by bruising and drying it; after which it is moulded into cakes according to fancy, and laid up for use. There is also a great abundance of cranberries, which proved very useful as an antiscorbutic.

We found also the whortleberry, chokecherries, gooseberries, and black currants with wild crab-apples: these last grow in clusters, are of small size and very tart. On the upper part of the river are found blackberries, hazel-nuts, acorns, &c. The country also possesses a great variety of nutritive roots: the natives make great use of those which have the virtue of curing or preventing the scurvy. We ate freely of them with the same intention, and with the same suc cess. One of these roots, which much resembles a small onion, serves them, in some sort, in place of cheese. Having gathered a sufficient quantity, they bake them with red-hot stones, until the steam ceases to ooze from the layer of grass and earth with which the roots are covered; then they pound them into a paste, and make the paste into loaves, of five or six pounds weight: the taste is not unlike liquorice, but not of so sickly a sweetness. When we made our first voyage up the river the natives gave us square biscuits, very well worked, and printed with different figures. These are made of a white root, pounded, reduced to paste, and dried in the sun. They call it *Chapaleel:* it is not very palatable, nor very nutritive.

But the principal food of the natives of the Columbia is fish. The salmon-fishery begins in July: that fish is here of an exquisite flavor, but it is extremely fat and oily; which renders it unwholesome for those who are not accustomed to it, and who eat too great a quantity: thus several of our people were attacked with diarrhœa in a few days after we began to make this fish our ordinary sustenance; but they found a remedy in the raspberries of the country which have an astringent property.

The months of August and September furnish excellent sturgeon. This fish varies exceedingly in size; I have seen some eleven feet long; and we took one that weighed, after the removal of the eggs and intestines, three hundred and ninety pounds. We took out nine gallons of roe. The sturgeon does not enter the river in so great quantities as the salmon.

In October and November we had salmon too, but of a quite different species—lean, dry and insipid. It differs from the other sort in form also; having very long teeth, and a hooked nose like the beak of a parrot. Our men termed it in derision "seven bark salmon," because it had almost no nutritive substance.

February brings a small fish about the size of a sardine. It has an exquisite flavor, and is taken in immense quantities, by means of a scoop net, which the Indians, seated in canoes, plunge into the schools: but the season is short, not even lasting two weeks.

The principal quadrupeds of the country are the elk, the black and white tailed deer; four species of bear, distinguished chiefly by the color of the fur or *poil*, to wit, the black, brown, white and grisly bear; the grisly bear is extremely ferocious; the white is found on the seashore toward the north; the wolf, the panther, the catamount, the lynx, the raccoon, the ground hog, opossum, mink, fisher, beaver, and the land and sea otter.* The sea otter has the handsomest fur that is known; the skin surpasses that of the land variety in size and in the beauty of the *poil;* the most esteemed color is the silver gray,

* Horses are abundant up the river; but they are not indigenous to the country. They will be spoken of in a future chapter.

which is highly prized in the Indies, and commands a great price.

The most remarkable birds are the eagle, the turkey-buzzard, the hawk, pelican, heron, gull, cormorant, crane, swan, and a great variety of wild ducks and geese. The pigeon, woodcock, and pheasant, are found in the forests as with us.

CHAPTER XIX.

Manners, Customs, Occupations, &c., of the Natives on the River Columbia.

THE natives inhabiting on the Columbia, from the mouth of that river to the falls, that is to say, on a space extending about 250 miles from east to west, are, generally speaking, of low stature, few of them passing five feet six inches, and many not even five feet. They pluck out the beard, in the manner of the other Indians of North America; but a few of the old men only suffer a tuft to grow upon their chins. On arriving among them we were exceedingly surprised to see that they had almost all flattened heads. This configuration is not a natural deformity, but an effect of art, caused by compression of the skull in infancy. It shocks strangers extremely, especially at first sight; nevertheless, among these barbarians it is an indispensable ornament: and when we signified to them how much this mode of flattening the forehead appeared to us to violate nature and good taste, they answered that it was only slaves who had not their heads flattened. The slaves, in fact, have the usual rounded head, and they are not permitted to flatten the foreheads of their children, destined to bear the chains of their sires. The natives of the Columbia procure these slaves from the neighboring tribes, and from the interior, in exchange for beads and furs. They treat them with humanity while their services are useful, but as soon as they become incapable of labor, neglect them and suffer them to perish of want. When dead, they throw their bodies, without ceremony, under the stump of an old decayed tree, or drag them to the woods to be devoured by the wolves and vultures.

The Indians of the Columbia are of a light copper color, active in body, and, above all, excellent swimmers. They are addicted to theft, or rather, they make no scruple of laying hands on whatever suits them in the property of strangers, whenever they can find an opportunity. The goods and effects of European manufacture are so precious in the eyes of these barbarians, that they rarely resist the temptation of stealing them.

These savages are not addicted to intemperance, unlike, in that respect the other American Indians, if we must not also except the Patagonians, who, like the Flatheads, regard intoxicating drinks as poisons, and drunkenness as disgraceful. I will relate a fact in point: one of the sons of the chief Comcomly being at the establishment one day, some of the gentlemen amused themselves with making him drink wine, and he was very soon drunk. He was sick in consequence, and remained in a state of stupor for two days. The old chief came to reproach us, saying that we had degraded his son by exposing him to the ridicule of the slaves, and besought us not to induce him to take strong liquors in future.

The men go entirely naked, not concealing any part of their bodies. Only in winter they throw over the shoulders a panther's skin, or else a sort of mantle made of the skins of wood-rats sewed together. In rainy weather I have seen them wear a mantle of rush mats, like a Roman toga, or the vestment which a priest wears in celebrating mass; thus equipped, and furnished with a conical hat made from fibrous roots and impermeable, they may call themselves rain-proof. The women, in addition to the mantle of skins, wear a petticoat made of the cedar bark, which they attach round the girdle, and which reaches to the middle of the thigh. It is a little longer behind than before, and is fabricated in the following manner: They strip off the fine bark of the cedar, soak it as one soaks hemp, and when it is drawn out into fibres, work it into a fringe; then with a strong cord they bind the fringes together. With so poor a vestment they contrive to satisfy the requirements of modesty; when they stand it drapes them fairly enough; and when they squat down in their manner, it falls between their legs, leaving nothing exposed but the bare knees and thighs. Some of the younger women twist the fibres of bark into small cords, knotted at the ends, and so form the petticoat, disposed in a fringe, like the first, but more easily kept clean and of better appearance.

Cleanliness is not a virtue among these females, who, in that respect, resemble the other Indian women of the continent. They anoint the body and dress the hair with fish oil, which does not diffuse an agreeable perfume. Their hair (which both sexes wear long) is jet black; it is badly combed, but parted in the middle, as is the custom of the sex everywhere, and kept shining by the fish-oil before-mentioned. Sometimes, in imitation of the men, they paint the whole body with a red earth mixed with fish-oil. Their ornaments consist of bracelets of brass, which they wear indifferently on the wrists and ankles; of strings of beads of different colors (they give a preference to the blue), and displayed in great profusion around the neck, and on the arms and legs; and of white shells, called *Haiqua*, which are their ordinary circulating medium. These shells are found beyond the straits of *Juan de Fuca*, and are from one to four inches long, and about half an inch in diameter: they are a little curved and naturally perforated: the longest are most valued. The price of all commodities is reckoned in these shells; a fathom string of the largest of them is worth about ten beaver-skins.

Although a little less slaves than the greater part of the Indian women elsewhere, the women on the Columbia are, nevertheless, charged with the most painful labors; they fetch water and wood, and carry the goods in their frequent changes of residence; they clean the fish and cut it up for drying; they prepare the food and cook the fruits in their season. Among their principal occupations is that of making rush mats, baskets for gathering roots, and hats very ingeniously wrought. As they want little clothing, they do not sew much, and the men have the needle in hand oftener than they.

The men are not lazy, especially during the fishing season. Not being hunters, and eating, consequently, little flesh-meat (although they are fond of it), fish makes, as I have observed, their principal diet. They profit, therefore, by the season when it is to be had, by taking as much as they can; knowing that the intervals will be periods of famine and abstinence, unless they provide sufficiently beforehand.

Their canoes are all made of cedar, and of a single trunk: we saw some which were five feet wide at midships, and thirty feet in length; these are the largest, and will carry from 25 to 30 men; the smallest will carry but two or three. The bows terminate in a very elongated point, running out four or five feet from the water line. It constitutes a separate piece, very ingeniously attached, and serves to break the surf in landing, or the wave on a rough sea. In landing they put the canoe round, so as to strike the beach stern on. Their oars or paddles are made of ash, and are about five feet long, with a broad blade, in the shape of an inverted crescent, and a cross at the top, like the handle of a crutch. The object of the crescent shape of the blade is to be able to draw it, edge-wise, through the water without making any noise, when they hunt the sea-otter, an animal which can only be caught when it is lying asleep on the rocks, and which has the sense of hearing very acute. All their canoes are painted red, and fancifully decorated.

Their houses, constructed of cedar, are remarkable for their form and size: some of them are one hundred feet in length by thirty or forty feet in width. They are constructed as follows: An oblong square of the intended size of the building is dug out to the depth of two or three feet; a double row of cedar posts is driven into the earth about ten feet apart; between these the planks are laid, overlapping each other to the requisite height. The roof is formed by a ridge-pole laid on taller posts, notched to receive it, and is constructed with rafters and planks laid clapboard-wise, and secured by cords for want of nails. When the house is designed for several families, there is a door for each, and a separate fireplace; the smoke escapes through an aperture formed by removing one of the boards of the roof. The door is low, of an oval shape, and is provided with a ladder, cut out of a log, to descend into the lodge. The entrance is generally effected stern-foremost.

The kitchen utensils consist of plates of ash-wood, bowls of fibrous roots, and a wooden kettle: with these they succeed in cooking their fish and meat in less time than we take with the help of pots and stewpans. See how they do it! Having heated a number of stones red-hot, they plunge them, one by one, in the vessel which is to contain the food to be prepared; as soon as the water boils, they put in the fish or meat, with some more heated stones on top, and cover up the whole with small rush mats, to retain the steam. In an incredibly short space of time the article is taken out and placed on a wooden platter, perfectly done and very palatable. The broth is taken out also, with a ladle of wood or horn.

It will be asked, no doubt, what instruments these savages use in the construction of their canoes and their houses. To cause their patience and industry to be admired as much as they deserve, it will be sufficient for me to mention that we did not find among them a single hatchet: their only tools consisted of an inch or half-inch chisel, usually made of an old file, and of a mallet, which was nothing but an oblong stone. With these wretched implements, and wedges made of hemlock knots, steeped in oil and hardened by the fire, they would undertake to cut down the largest cedars of the forest, to dig them out and fashion them into canoes, to split them, and get out the boards wherewith to build their houses. Such achievements with such means, are a marvel of ingenuity and patience.

CHAPTER XX.

Manners and Customs of the Natives continued.—Their Wars.—Their Marriages.—Medicine Men.—Funeral Ceremonies.—Religious Notions.—Language.

THE politics of the natives of the Columbia are a simple affair: each village has its chief, but that chief does not seem to exercise a great authority over his fellow-citizens. Nevertheless, at his death, they pay him great honors: they use a kind of mourning, which consists in painting the face with black, in lieu of gay colors; they chant his funeral song or oration for a whole month. The chiefs are considered in proportion to their riches: such a chief has a great many wives, slaves, and strings of beads—he is accounted a great chief. These barbarians approach in that respect to certain civilized nations, among whom the worth of a man is estimated by the quantity of gold he possesses.

As all the villages form so many independent sovereignties, differences sometimes arise, whether between the chiefs or the tribes. Ordinarily, these terminate by compensations equivalent to the injury. But when the latter is of a grave character, like a murder (which is rare), or the abduction of a woman (which is very common), the parties, having made sure of a number of young braves to aid them, prepare for war. Before commencing hostilities, however, they give notice of the day when they will proceed to attack the hostile village; not following in that respect the custom of almost all other American Indians, who are wont to burst upon their enemy unawares, and to massacre or carry off men, women, and children; these people, on the contrary, embark in their canoes, which on these occasions are paddled by the women, repair to the hostile village, enter into parley, and do all they can to terminate the affair amicably: sometimes a third party becomes mediator between the first two, and of course observes an exact neutrality. If those who seek justice do not obtain it to their satisfaction, they retire to some distance, and the combat begins, and is continued for some time with fury on both sides; but as soon as one or two men are killed, the party which has lost these, owns itself beaten and the battle ceases. If it is the people of the village attacked who are worsted, the others do not retire without receiving presents. When the conflict is postponed till the next day (for they never fight but in open daylight, as if to render nature witness of their exploits), they keep up frightful cries all night long, and, when they are sufficiently near to understand each other, defy one another by menaces, railleries, and sarcasms, like the heroes of Homer and Virgil. The women and children are always removed from the village before the action.

Their combats are almost all maritime: for they fight ordinarily in their pirogues, which they take care to careen, so as to present the broadside to the enemy, and half lying down, avoid the greater part of the arrows let fly at them.

But the chief reason of the bloodlessness of

their combats is the inefficiency of their offensive weapons, and the excellence of their defensive armor. Their offensive arms are merely a bow and arrow, and a kind of double-edged sabre, about two and a half feet long, and six inches wide in the blade: they rarely come to sufficiently close quarters to make use of the last. For defensive armor they wear a cassock or tunic of elk-skin double, descending to the ankles, with holes for the arms. It is impenetrable by their arrows, which can not pierce two thicknesses of leather; and as their heads are also covered with a sort of helmet, the neck is almost the only part in which they can be wounded. They have another kind of corslet, made like the corsets of our ladies, of splinters of hard wood interlaced with nettle twine. The warrior who wears this cuirass does not use the tunic of elk-skin; he is consequently less protected, but a great deal more free; the said tunic being very heavy and very stiff.

It is almost useless to observe that, in their military expeditions, they have their bodies and faces daubed with different paints, often of the most extravagant designs. I remember to have seen a war-chief, with one exact half of his face painted white and the other half black.

Their marriages are conducted with a good deal of ceremony. When a young man seeks a girl in marriage, his parents make the proposals to those of the intended bride, and when it has been agreed upon what presents the future bridegroom is to offer to the parents of the bride, all parties assemble at the house of the latter, whither the neighbors are invited to witness the contract. The presents, which consist of slaves, strings of beads, copper bracelets, *haiqua* shells, &c., are distributed by the young man, who, on his part receives as many, and sometimes more, according to the means or the munificence of the parents of his betrothed. The latter is then led forward by the old matrons and presented to the young man, who takes her as his wife, and all retire to their quarters.

The men are not very scrupulous in their choice, and take small pains to inform themselves what conduct a young girl has observed before her nuptials; and it must be owned that few marriages would take place, if the youth would only espouse maidens without reproach on the score of chastity; for the unmarried girls are by no means scrupulous in that particular, and their parents give them, on that head, full liberty. But once the marriage is contracted, the spouses observe toward each other an inviolable fidelity; adultery is almost unknown among them, and the woman who should be guilty of it would be punished with death. At the same time, the husband may repudiate his wife, and the latter may then unite herself in marriage to another man. Polygamy is permitted, indeed is customary; there are some who have as many as four or five wives; and although it often happens that the husband loves one better than the rest, they never show any jealousy, but live together in the most perfect concord.*

* This appears improbable, and is, no doubt, overstated; but so far as it is true, only shows the degradation of these women, and the absence of moral love on both sides. The indifference to virgin chastity described by Mr. F., is a characteristic of barbar-

There are charlatans everywhere, but they are more numerous among savages than anywhere else, because among these ignorant and superstitious people the trade is at once more profitable and less dangerous. As soon as a native of the Columbia is indisposed, no matter what the malady, they send for the medicine man, who treats the patient in the absurd manner usually adopted by these impostors, and with such violence of manipulation, that often a sick man, whom a timely bleeding or purgative would have saved, is carried off by a sudden death.

They deposite their dead in canoes, on rocks sufficiently elevated not to be overflowed by the spring freshets. By the side of the dead are laid his bow, his arrows, and some of his fishing

ous nations in general, and is explained by the principle stated in the next note below; the savage state being essentially one in which the supernatural bond of human fellowship is snapped: it is (as it has been called) the state of *nature*, in which continence is practically impossible; and what men can not have, that they soon cease to prize. The same utter indifference to the past conduct of the girls they marry is mentioned by MAYHEW as existing among the costermongers and street population of London, whom he well likens to the barbarous tribes lying on the outskirts of more ancient nations.—ED.

implements; if it is a woman, her beads and bracelets: the wives, the relatives and the slaves of the defunct cut their hair in sign of grief, and for several days, at the rising and setting of the sun, go to some distance from the village to chant a funeral song.

These people have not, properly speaking, a public worship.* I could never perceive, during my residence among them, that they worshipped any idol. They had, nevertheless, some small sculptured figures; but they appeared to hold them in light esteem, offering to barter them for trifles.

Having travelled with one of the sons of the chief of the Chinooks (Comcomly), an intelligent and communicative young man, I put to him several questions touching their religious belief, and

* It is Coleridge who observes that *every tribe is barbarous* which has no recognised public worship or cult, and no regular priesthood as opposed to self-constituted conjurors. It is, in fact, by public worship alone that human society is organized and vivified; and it is impossible to maintain such worship without a sacerdotal order, however it be constituted. *No culture without a cult*, is the result of the study of the races of mankind. Hence those who would destroy religion are the enemies of civilization.—ED.

the following is, in substance, what he told me respecting it: Men, according to their ideas, were created by a divinity whom they name *Etalapass;* but they were imperfect, having a mouth that was not opened, eyes that were fast closed, hands and feet that were not moveable; in a word, they were rather statues of flesh, than living men. A second divinity, whom they call *Ecannum*, less powerful, but more benign than the former, having seen men in their state of imperfection, took a sharp stone and laid open their mouths and eyes; he gave agility, also, to their feet, and motion to their hands. This compassionate divinity was not content with conferring these first benefits; he taught men to make canoes, paddles, nets, and, in a word, all the tools and instruments they use. He did still more: he threw great rocks into the river, to obstruct the ascent of the salmon, in order that they might take as many as they wanted.

The natives of the Columbia further believe, that the men who have been good citizens, good fathers, good husbands, and good fishermen, who have not committed murder, &c., will be perfectly happy after their death, and will go to a country where they will find fish, fruit, &c., in abundance; and that, on the contrary, those who have lived wickedly, will inhabit a country of fasting and want, where they will eat nothing but bitter roots, and have nothing to drink but salt water.

If these notions in regard to the origin and future destiny of man are not exactly conformed to sound reason or to divine revelation, it will be allowed that they do not offer the absurdities with which the mythologies of many ancient nations abound.* The article which makes skill in fishing a virtue worthy of being compensated in the other world, does not disfigure the salutary and consoling dogma of the immortality of the

* It seems clear that this Indian mythology is a form of the primitive tradition obscured by symbol. The creation of man by the Supreme Divinity, but in an imperfect state ("his eyes not yet opened"), his deliverance from that condition by an inferior but more beneficent deity (the Satan of the Bible), and the progress of the emancipated and enlightened being, in the arts of industry, are clearly set forth. Thus the devil has his cosmogony as well as the Almighty, and his tradition in opposition to the divine.—Ed.

soul, and that of future rewards and punishments, so much as one is at first tempted to think; for if we reflect a little, we shall discover that the skilful fisherman, in laboring for himself, labors also for society; he is a useful citizen, who contributes, as much as lies in his power, to avert from his fellow-men the scourge of famine; he is a religious man, who honors the divinity by making use of his benefits. Surely a great deal of the theology of a future life prevalent among civilized men, does not excel this in profundity.

It is not to be expected that men perfectly ignorant, like these Indians, should be free from superstitions: one of the most ridiculous they have, regards the method of preparing and eating fish. In the month of July, 1811, the natives brought us at first a very scanty supply of the fresh salmon, from the fear that we would cut the fish crosswise instead of lengthwise; being persuaded that if we did so, the river would be obstructed, and the fishing ruined. Having reproached the chief on that account, they brought us a greater quantity, but all cooked, and which, not to displease them, it was necessary to eat before sunset. Re-assured at last by our solemn promises not to cut the fish crosswise, they supplied us abundantly during the remainder of the season.

In spite of the vices that may be laid to the charge of the natives of the Columbia, I regard them as nearer to a state of civilization than any of the tribes who dwell east of the Rocky mountains. They did not appear to me so attached to their customs that they could not easily adopt those of civilized nations: they would dress themselves willingly in the European mode, if they had the means. To encourage this taste, we lent pantaloons to the chiefs who visited us, when they wished to enter our houses, never allowing them to do it in a state of nudity. They possess, in an eminent degree, the qualities opposed to indolence, improvidence, and stupidity: the chiefs, above all, are distinguished for their good sense and intelligence. Generally speaking, they have a ready intellect and a tenacious memory. Thus old Comcomly recognised the mate of the *Al-*

batross as having visited the country sixteen years before, and recalled to the latter the name of the captain under whom he had sailed at that period.

The *Chinook* language is spoken by all the nations from the mouth of the Columbia to the falls. It is hard and difficult to pronounce, for strangers; being full of gutturals, like the Gaelic. The combinations *thl*, or *tl*, and *lt*, are as frequent in the Chinook as in the Mexican.*

* There can not be a doubt that the existing tribes on the N. W. coast, have reached that country from the *South*, and not from the North. They are the *debris* of the civilization of Central America, expelled by a defecating process that is going on in all human societies, and so have sunk into barbarism.—Ed

CHAPTER XXI.

Departure from Astoria or Fort George.—Accident.—Passage of the Dalles or Narrows.—Great Columbian Desert.—Aspect of the Country.—Wallawalla and Shaptin Rivers.—Rattlesnakes.—Some Details regarding the Natives of the Upper Columbia.

We quitted Fort George (or Astoria, if you please) on Monday morning, the 4th of April, 1814, in ten canoes, five of which were of bark and five of cedar wood, carrying each seven men as crew, and two passengers, in all ninety persons, and all well armed. Messrs. J. G. M'Tavish, D. Stuart, J. Clarke, B. Pillet, W. Wallace, D. M'Gillis, D. M'Kenzie, &c., were of the party. Nothing remarkable occurred to us as far as the first falls, which we reached on the 10th. The portage was effected immediately, and we encamped on an island for the night. Our numbers had caused the greater part of the natives to take to flight, and those who remained in the villages showed the most pacific dispositions. They sold us four horses and thirty dogs, which were immediately slaughtered for food.

We resumed our route on the 11th, at an early hour. The wind was favorable, but blew with violence. Toward evening, the canoe in which Mr. M'Tavish was, in doubling a point of rock, was run under by its press of sail, and sunk. Happily the river was not deep at this place; no one was drowned; and we succeeded in saving all the goods. This accident compelled us to camp at an early hour.

On the 12th, we arrived at a rapid called the *Dalles*: this is a channel cut by nature through the rocks, which are here almost perpendicular: the channel is from 150 to 300 feet wide, and about two miles long. The whole body of the river rushes through it, with great violence, and renders navigation impracticable. The portage occupied us till dusk. Although we had not seen a single Indian in the course of the day, we kept sentinels on duty all night: for it was here that Messrs. Stuart and Reed were attacked by the natives.

On the 13th, we made two more portages, and met Indians, of whom we purchased horses and wood. We camped early on a sandy plain, where we passed a bad night; the wind, which blew violently, raised clouds of sand, which incommoded us greatly, and spoiled every mouthful of food we took.

On the 14th and 15th, we passed what are called the Great Plains of the Columbia. From the top of the first rapid to this point, the aspect of the country becomes more and more *triste* and disagreeable; one meets at first nothing but bare hills, which scarcely offer a few isolated pines, at a great distance from each other; after that, the earth, stripped of verdure, does not afford you the sight of a single shrub; the little grass which grows in that arid soil, appears burnt by the rigor of the climate. The natives who frequent the banks of the river, for the salmon fishery, have no other wood but that which they take floating down. We passed several rapids, and a small stream called Utalah, which flows from the southeast.

On the 16th, we found the river narrowed; the banks rose on either side in elevations, without, however, offering a single tree. We reached the river *Wallawalla*, which empties into the Columbia on the southeast. It is narrow at its confluence, and is not navigable for any great distance. A range of mountains was visible to the S. E., about fifty or sixty miles off. Behind these mountains the country becomes again flat and sandy, and is inhabited by a tribe called the *Snakes*. We found on the left bank of the *Wallawalla*, an encampment of Indians, consisting of about twenty lodges. They sold us six dogs and eight horses, the greater part extremely lean. We killed two of the horses immediately: I mounted one of the six that remained; Mr. Ross took another; and we drove the other four before us. Toward the decline of day we passed the river *Lewis*, called, in the language of the country, the *Sha-ap-tin*. It comes from the S. E., and is the same that Lewis and Clarke descended in 1805. The *Sha-ap-tin* appeared to me to have little depth, and to be about 300 yards wide, at its confluence.

The country through which we were now passing, was a mingling of hills, steep rocks, and valleys covered with wormwood; the stems of which shrub are nearly six inches thick, and might serve for fuel. We killed six rattlesnakes on the 15th, and on the 16th saw a great many more among the rocks. These dangerous reptiles appeared to be very numerous in this part of the country. The plains are also inhabited by a little quadruped, only about eight or nine inches in length, and approaching the dog in form. These animals have the hair, or *poil*, of a reddish brown, and strong fore-paws, armed with long claws which serve them to dig out their holes under the earth. They have a great deal of curiosity: as soon as they hear a noise they come out of their holes and bark. They are not vicious, but, though easily tamed, can not be domesticated.

The natives of the upper Columbia, beginning at the falls, differ essentially in language, manners, and habits, from those of whom I have spoken in the preceding chapters. They do not dwell in villages, like the latter, but are nomads, like the Tartars and the Arabs of the desert: their women are more industrious, and the young girls more reserved and chaste than those of the populations lower down. They do not go naked, but both sexes wear habits made of dressed deer-skin, which they take care to rub with chalk, to keep them clean and white. They are almost always seen on horseback, and are in general good riders; they pursue the deer and penetrate even to Missouri, to kill buffalo, the flesh of which they dry, and bring it back on their horses, to make their principal food during the winter. These expeditions are not free from danger; for they have a great deal to apprehend from the *Black-feet*, who are their enemies. As this last tribe is powerful and ferocious, the *Snakes*, the *Pierced-noses* or *Sha-ap-tins*, the *Flatheads*, &c., make common cause against them, when the former go to hunt east of the mountains. They set out with their families, and the cavalcade often numbers two thousand horses. When they have the good fortune not to encounter the enemy, they return with the spoils of an abundant chase; they load a part of their horses with the hides and beef, and return home to pass the winter in peace. Sometimes, on the contrary, they are so harassed by the Blackfeet, who surprise them in the night and carry off their horses, that they are forced to return light-handed, and then they have nothing to eat but roots, all the winter.

These Indians are passionately fond of horse-races: by the bets they make on these occasions they sometimes lose all that they possess. The women ride, as well as the men. For a bridle they use a cord of horse-hair, which they attach round the animal's mouth; with that he is easily checked, and by laying the hand on his neck, is made to wheel to this side or that. The saddle is a cushion of stuffed deer-skin, very suitable for the purpose to which it is destined, rarely hurting the horse, and not fatiguing the rider so much as our European saddles. The stirrups are pieces of hard wood, ingeniously wrought, and of the same shape as those which are used in civilized countries. They are covered with a piece of deer-skin, which is sewed on wet, and in drying stiffens and becomes hard and firm. The saddles for women differ in form, being furnished with the antlers of a deer, so as to resemble the high pommelled saddle of the Mexican ladies.

They procure their horses from the herds of these animals which are found in a wild state in the country extending between the northern latitudes and the gulf of Mexico, and which sometimes count a thousand or fifteen hundred in a troop. These horses come from New Mexico, and are of Spanish race. We even saw some which had been marked with a hot iron by Spaniards. Some of our men, who had been at the south, told me that they had seen among the Indians, bridles, the bits of which were of silver. The form of the saddles used by the females, proves that they have taken their pattern from the Spanish ones destined for the same use. One of the partners of the N. W. Company (Mr. M'Tavish) assured us that he had seen among the *Spokans*, an old woman who told him that she had seen men ploughing the earth; she told him that she had also seen churches, which she made him understand by imitating the sound of a bell and the action of pulling a bell-rope; and further to confirm her account, made the sign of the cross. That gentleman concluded that she had been made prisoner and sold to the Spaniards on the *Del Norte;* but I think it more probable it was nearer, in North California, at the mission of *San Carlos* or *San Francisco.*

As the manner of taking wild horses should not be generally known to my readers, I will relate it here in few words. The Indian who wishes to capture some horses, mounts one of his fleetest coursers, being armed with a long cord of horsehair, one end of which is attached to his saddle, and the other is a running noose. Arrived at the herd, he dashes into the midst of it, and flinging his cord, or *lasso*, passes it dexterously over the head of the animal he selects;

then wheeling his courser, draws the cord after him; the wild horse, finding itself strangling, makes little resistance; the Indian then approaches, ties his fore and hind legs together, and leaves him till he has taken in this manner as many as he can. He then drives them home before him, and breaks them in at leisure.

CHAPTER XXII.

Meeting with the Widow of a Hunter.—Her Narrative.—Reflections of the Author.—Priest's Rapid.—River Okenakan.—Kettle Falls.—Pine Moss.—Scarcity of Food.—Rivers, Lakes, &c.—Accident.—A Rencontre.—First View of the Rocky Mountains.

On the 17th, the fatigue I had experienced the day before, on horseback, obliged me to re-embark in my canoe. About eight o'clock, we passed a little river flowing from the N. W. We perceived, soon after, three canoes, the persons in which were struggling with their paddles to overtake us. As we were still pursuing our way, we heard a child's voice cry out in French —"*arrêtez donc, arrêtez donc*"—(stop! stop!). We put ashore, and the canoes having joined us, we perceived in one of them the wife and children of a man named *Pierre Dorion*, a hunter, who had been sent on with a party of eight, under the command of Mr. J. Reed, among the *Snakes*, to join there the hunters left by Messrs. Hunt and Crooks, near Fort Henry, and to secure horses and provisions for our journey. This woman informed us, to our no small dismay, of the tragical fate of all those who composed that party. She told us that in the month of January, the hunters being dispersed here and there, setting their traps for the beaver, Jacob Regner, Gilles Leclerc, and Pierre Dorion, her husband, had been attacked by the natives. Leclerc, having been mortally wounded, reached her tent or hut, where he expired in a few minutes, after having announced to her that her husband had been killed. She immediately took two horses that were near the lodge, mounted her two boys upon them, and fled in all haste to the wintering house of Mr. Reed, which was about five days' march from the spot where her husband fell. Her horror and disappointment were extreme, when she found the house—a log cabin—deserted, and on drawing nearer, was soon convinced, by the traces of blood, that Mr. Reed also had been murdered. No time was to be lost in lamentations, and she had immediately fled toward the mountains south of the *Wallawalla*, where, being impeded by the depth of the snow, she was forced to winter, having killed both the horses to subsist herself and her children. But at last, finding herself out of provisions, and the snow beginning to melt, she had crossed the mountains with her boys, hoping to find some more humane Indians, who would let her live among them till the boats from the fort below should be ascending the river in the spring, and so reached the banks of the Columbia, by the Wallawalla. Here, indeed, the natives had received her with much hospitality, and it was the Indians of Wallawalla who brought her to us. We made them some presents to repay their care and pains, and they returned well satisfied.

The persons who lost their lives in this unfortunate wintering party, were Mr. John Reed, (clerk), Jacob Regner, John Hubbough, Pierre Dorion (hunters), Gilles Leclerc, François Landry, J. B. Turcotte, André la Chapelle and Pierre

De Launay, (*voyageurs*).* We had no doubt that this massacre was an act of vengeance, on the part of the natives, in retaliation for the death of one of their people, whom Mr. John Clark had hanged for theft the spring before. This fact, the massacre on the Tonquin, the unhappy end of Captain Cook, and many other similar examples, prove how carefully the Europeans, who have relations with a barbarous people, should abstain from acting in regard to them on the footing of too marked an inequality, and especially from punishing their offences according to usages and codes, in which there is too often an enormous disproportion between the crime and the punishment. If these pretended exemplary punishments seem to have a good effect at first sight, they almost always produce terrible consequences in the sequel.

On the 18th, we passed *Priest's Rapid*, so named by Mr. Stuart and his people, who saw at

* Turcotte died of *King's Evil.* De Launay was a half-breed, of violent temper, who had taken an Indian woman to live with him; he left Mr. Reed in the autumn, and was never heard of again.

this spot, in 1811, as they were ascending the river, a number of savages, one of whom was performing on the rest certain aspersions and other ceremonies, which had the air of being coarse imitations of the Catholic worship. For our part, we met here some Indians of whom we bought two horses. The banks of the river at this place are tolerably high, but the country back of them is flat and uninteresting.

On the 20th, we arrived at a place where the bed of the river is extremely contracted, and where we were obliged to make a portage. Messrs. J. Stuart and Clarke left us here, to proceed on horseback to the Spokan trading house, to procure there the provisions which would be necessary for us, in order to push on to the mountains.

On the 21st, we lightened of their cargoes, three canoes, in which those who were to cross the continent embarked, to get on with greater speed. We passed several rapids, and began to see mountains covered with snow.

On the 22d, we began to see some pines on

the ridge of the neighboring hills; and at evening we encamped under *trees*, a thing which had not happened to us since the 12th.

On the 23d, toward 9, A. M., we reached the trading post established by D. Stuart, at the mouth of the river *Okenakan*. The spot appeared to us charming, in comparison with the country through which we had journeyed for twelve days past: the two rivers here meeting, and the immense prairies covered with a fine verdure, strike agreeably the eye of the observer; but there is not a tree or a shrub to diversify the scene, and render it a little less naked and less monotonous. We found here Messrs. J. M'Gillivray and Ross, and Mr. O. de Montigny, who had taken service with the N. W. Company, and who charged me with a letter for his brother.

Toward midday we re-embarked, to continue our journey. After having passed several dangerous rapids without accident, always through a country broken by shelving rocks, diversified with hills and verdant prairies, we arrived, on the 29th, at the portage of the *Chaudieres* or

Kettle falls. This is a fall where the water precipitates itself over an immense rock of white marble, veined with red and green, that traverses the bed of the river from N. W. to S. E. We effected the portage immediately, and encamped on the edge of a charming prairie.

We found at this place some Indians who had been fasting, they assured us, for several days. They appeared, in fact, reduced to the most pitiable state, having nothing left but skin and bones, and scarcely able to drag themselves along, so that not without difficulty could they even reach the margin of the river, to get a little water to wet their parched lips. It is a thing that often happens to these poor people, when their chase has not been productive; their principal nourishment consisting, in that case, of the pine moss, which they boil till it is reduced to a sort of glue or black paste, of a sufficient consistence to take the form of biscuit. I had the curiosity to taste this bread, and I thought I had got in my mouth a bit of soap. Yet some of our people, who had been reduced to eat this glue, assured me that when fresh made it had a very good taste, seasoned with meat.* We partly relieved these wretched natives from our scanty store.

On the 30th, while we were yet encamped at Kettle falls, Messrs. J. Stuart and Clarke arrived from the post at Spokan. The last was mounted on the finest-proportioned gray charger, full seventeen hands high, that I had seen in these parts: Mr. Stuart had got a fall from his, in trying to urge him, and had hurt himself severely. These gentlemen not having brought us the provisions we expected, because the hunters who had been sent for that purpose among the *Flatheads*, had not been able to procure any, it was resolved to divide our party, and that Messrs. M'Donald, J. Stuart, and M'Kenzie should go forward to the post situated east of the mountains, in order to send us thence horses and supplies. These gentlemen quitted us on the 1st of May. After their

* The process of boiling employed by the Indians in this case, extracts from the moss its gelatine, which serves to supply the waste of those tissues into which that principle enters; but as the moss contains little or none of the proximates which constitute the bulk of the living solids and fluids, it will not, of course, by itself, support life or strength.—ED.

departure we killed two horses and dried the meat; which occupied us the rest of that day and all the next. In the evening of the 2d, Mr. A. Stuart arrived at our camp. He had recovered from his wounds (received in the conflict with the natives, before related), and was on his way to his old wintering place on *Slave lake*, to fetch his family to the Columbia.

We resumed our route on the morning of the 3d of May, and went to encamp that evening at the upper-end of a rapid, where we began to descry mountains covered with forests, and where the banks of the river themselves were low and thinly timbered.

On the 4th, after having passed several considerable rapids, we reached the confluence of *Flathead* river. This stream comes from the S. E., and falls into the Columbia in the form of a cascade: it may be one hundred and fifty yards wide at its junction.

On the morning of the 5th, we arrived at the confluence of the *Coutonais* river. This stream also flows from the south, and has nearly the same width as the *Flathead.* Shortly after passing it, we entered a lake or enlargement of the river, which we crossed to encamp at its upper extremity. This lake may be thirty or forty miles, and about four wide at its broadest part: it is surrounded by lofty hills, which for the most part have their base at the water's edge, and rise by gradual and finely-wooded terraces, offering a sufficiently pretty view.

On the 6th, after we had run through a narrow strait or channel some fifteen miles long, we entered another lake, of less extent than the former but equally picturesque. When we were nearly in the middle of it, an accident occurred which, if not very disastrous, was sufficiently singular. One of the men, who had been on the sick-list for several days, requested to be landed for an instant. Not being more than a mile from the shore, we acceded to his request, and made accordingly for a projecting head-land; but when we were about three hundred or four hundred yards from the point, the canoe struck with force against the trunk of a tree which was planted in the bottom of the lake, and the extremity of which barely reached the surface of the water.* It needed no more to break a hole in so frail a vessel; the canoe was pierced through the bottom and filled in a trice; and despite all our efforts we could not get off the tree, which had penetrated two or three feet within her; perhaps that was our good fortune, for the opening was at least a yard long. One of the men, who was an expert swimmer, stripped, and was about to go ashore with an axe lashed to his back, to make a raft for us, when the other canoe, which had been proceeding up the lake, and was a mile ahead, perceived our signals of distress, and came to our succor. They carried us to land, where it was necessary to encamp forthwith, as well to dry ourselves as to mend the canoe.

On the 7th, Mr. A. Stuart, whom we had left behind at Kettle falls, came up with us, and we pursued our route in company. Toward evening

* A *snag* of course, of the nature of which the young Canadian seems to have been ignorant.

we met natives, camped on the bank of the river: they gave us a letter from which we learned that Mr. M'Donald and his party had passed there on the 4th. The women at this camp were busy spinning the coarse wool of the mountain sheep: they had blankets or mantles, woven or platted of the same material, with a heavy fringe all round: I would gladly have purchased one of these, but as we were to carry all our baggage on our backs across the mountains, was forced to relinquish the idea. Having bought of these savages some pieces of dried venison, we pursued our journey. The country began to be ascending; the stream was very rapid; and we made that day little progress.

On the 8th we began to see snow on the shoals or sand-banks of the river: the atmosphere grew very cold. The banks on either side presented only high hills covered to the top with impenetrable forests. While the canoes were working up a considerable rapid, I climbed the hills with Mr. M'Gillis, and we walked on, following the course of the river, some five or six miles. The snow was very deep in the ravines or narrow gorges which are found between the bases of the hills. The most common trees are the Norway pine and the cedar: the last is here, as on the borders of the sea, of a prodigious size.

On the 9th and 10th, as we advanced but slowly, the country presented the same aspect as on the 8th. Toward evening of the 10th, we perceived a-head of us a chain of high mountains entirely covered with snow. The bed of the river was hardly more than sixty yards wide, and was filled with dry banks composed of coarse gravel and small pebble.

CHAPTER XXIII.

Course of the Columbia River.—Canoe River.—Foot-march toward the Rocky Mountains.—Passage of the Mountains.

On the 11th, that is to say, one month, day for day, after our departure from the falls, we quitted the Columbia, to enter a little stream to which Mr. Thompson had given, in 1811, the name of *Canoe* river, from the fact that it was on this fork that he constructed the canoes which carried him to the Pacific.

The Columbia, which in the portion above the falls (not taking into consideration some local sinuosities) comes from the N. N. E., takes a bend here so that the stream appears to flow from the S. E.* Some boatmen, and particularly Mr.

* Mr. Franchere uniformly mentions the direction from which a stream appears to flow, not that toward which it runs; a natural method on the part of one who was ascending the current.

Regis Bruguier, who had ascended that river to its source, informed me that it came out of two small lakes, not far from the chain of the Rocky Mountains, which, at that place, diverges considerably to the east. According to Arrowsmith's map, the course of the *Tacoutche Tessé*, from its mouth in the Pacific Ocean, to its source in the Rocky mountains, is about twelve hundred English miles, or four hundred French leagues of twenty-five to a degree; that is to say, from two hundred and forty to two hundred and eighty miles from west to east, from its mouth to the first falls: seven hundred and fifty miles nearly from S. S. W. to N. N. E., from the first rapids to the bend at the confluence of *Canoe* river; and one hundred and fifty or one hundred and eighty miles from that confluence to its source. We were not provided with the necessary instruments to determine the latitude, and still less the longitude, of our different stations; but it took us four or five days to go up from the factory at Astoria to the falls, and we could not have made less than sixty miles a day: and, as I have just remarked, we occupied an entire month in getting from the falls to Canoe river: deducting four or five days, on which we did not travel, there remain twenty-five days march; and it is not possible that we made less than thirty miles a day, one day with another.

We ascended Canoe river to the point where it ceases to be navigable, and encamped in the same place where Mr. Thompson wintered in 1810–'11. We proceeded immediately to secure our canoes, and to divide the baggage among the men, giving each fifty pounds to carry, including his provisions. A sack of *pemican*, or pounded meat, which we found in a *cache*, where it had been left for us, was a great acquisition, as our supplies were nearly exhausted.

On the 12th we began our foot march to the mountains, being twenty-four in number, rank and file. Mr. A. Stuart remained at the portage to bestow in a place of safety the effects which we could not carry, such as boxes, kegs, camp-kettles, &c. We traversed first some swamps, next a dense bit of forest, and then we found ourselves marching up the gravelly banks of the little *Canoe* river. Fatigue obliged us to camp early.

On the 13th we pursued our journey, and entered into the valleys between the mountains, where there lay not less than four or five feet of snow. We were obliged to ford the river ten or a dozen times in the course of the day, sometimes with the water up to our necks. These frequent fordings were rendered necessary by abrupt and steep rocks or bluffs, which it was impossible to get over without plunging into the wood for a great distance. The stream being very swift, and rushing over a bed of stones, one of the men fell and lost a sack containing our last piece of salt pork, which we were preserving as a most precious treasure. The circumstances in which we found ourselves made us regard this as a most unfortunate accident. We encamped that night at the foot of a steep mountain, and sent on Mr. Pillet and the guide, M'Kay, to hasten a supply of provisions to meet us.

On the morning of the 14th we began to climb

the mountain which we had before us. We were obliged to stop every moment, to take breath, so stiff was the ascent. Happily it had frozen hard the night before, and the crust of the snow was sufficient to bear us. After two or three hours of incredible exertions and fatigues, we arrived at the *plateau* or summit, and followed the foot-prints of those who had preceded us. This mountain is placed between two others a great deal more elevated, compared with which it is but a hill, and of which, indeed, it is only, as it were, the valley. Our march soon became fatiguing, on account of the depth of the snow, which, softened by the rays of the sun, could no longer bear us as in the morning. We were obliged to follow exactly the traces of those who had preceded us, and to plunge our legs up to the knees in the holes they had made, so that it was as if we had put on and taken off, at every step, a very large pair of boots. At last we arrived at a good hard bottom, and a clear space, which our guide said was a little lake frozen over, and here we stopped for the night. This lake, or rather these lakes (for there are two) are situated in the midst of the valley or *cup* of the mountains. On either side were immense glaciers, or ice-bound rocks, on which the rays of the setting sun reflected the most beautiful prismatic colors. One of these icy peaks was like a fortress of rock; it rose perpendicularly some fifteen or eighteen hundred feet above the level of the lakes, and had the summit covered with ice. Mr. J. Henry, who first discovered the pass, gave this extraordinary rock the name of *McGillivray's Rock*, in honor of one of the partners of the N. W. Company. The lakes themselves are not much over three or four hundred yards in circuit, and not over two hundred yards apart. Canoe river, which, as we have already seen, flows to the west, and falls into the Columbia, takes its rise in one of them; while the other gives birth to one of the branches of the *Athabasca*, which runs first eastward, then northward, and which, after its junction with the *Unjighah*, north of the Lake of the Mountains, takes the name of *Slave* river, as far the lake of that name, and afterward that of

M'Kenzie river, till it empties into, or is lost in, the Frozen ocean. Having cut a large pile of wood, and having, by tedious labor for nearly an hour, got through the ice to the clear water of the lake on which we were encamped, we supped frugally on pounded maize, arranged our bivouac, and passed a pretty good night, though it was bitterly cold. The most common wood of the locality was cedar and stunted pine. The heat of our fire made the snow melt, and by morning the embers had reached the solid ice: the depth from the snow surface was about five feet.

On the 15th, we continued our route, and soon began to descend the mountain. At the end of three hours, we reached the banks of a stream—the outlet of the second lake above mentioned—here and there frozen over, and then again tumbling down over rock and pebbly bottom in a thousand fantastic gambols; and very soon we had to ford it. After a tiresome march, by an extremely difficult path in the midst of woods, we encamped in the evening under some cypresses. I had hit my right knee against the branch of a fallen tree on the first day of our march, and now began to suffer acutely with it. It was impossible, however, to flinch, as I must keep up with the party or be left to perish.

On the 16th, our path lay through thick swamps and forest; we recrossed the small stream we had forded the day before, and our guide conducted us to the banks of the *Athabasca*, which we also forded. As this passage was the last to be made, we dried our clothes, and pursued our journey through a more agreeable country than on the preceding days. In the evening we camped on the margin of a verdant plain, which, the guide informed us, was called *Coro prairie*. We had met in the course of the day several buffalo tracks, and a number of the bones of that quadruped bleached by time. Our flesh-meat having given out entirely, our supper consisted in some handfuls of corn, which we parched in a pan.

We resumed our route very early on the 17th, and after passing a forest of trembling poplar or aspen, we again came in sight of the river which we had left the day before. Arriving then at an elevated promontory or cape, our guide made us turn back in order to pass it at its most accessible point. After crossing it, not without difficulty, we soon came upon fresh horse-prints, a sure indication that there were some of those animals in our neighborhood. Emerging from the forest, each took the direction which he thought would lead soonest to an encampment. We all presently arrived at an old house which the traders of the N. W. Company had once constructed, but which had been abandoned for some four or five years. The site of this trading post is the most charming that can be imagined: suffice to say that it is built on the bank of the beautiful river *Athabasca*, and is surrounded by green and smiling prairies and superb woodlands. Pity there is nobody there to enjoy these rural beauties and to praise, while admiring them, the Author of Nature. We found there Mr. Pillet, and one of Mr. J. M'Donald's party, who had his leg broken by the kick of a horse. After regaling ourselves with *pemican* and some fresh venison, we set out again, leaving two of the party to take care of the lame man, and went on about eight or nine miles farther to encamp.

On the 18th, we had rain. I took the lead, and after having walked about ten or twelve miles, on the slope of a mountain denuded of trees, I perceived some smoke issuing from a tuft of trees in the bottom of a valley, and near the river. I descended immediately, and reached a small camp, where I found two men who were coming to meet us with four horses. I made them fire off two guns as a signal to the rest of our people who were coming up in the rear, and presently we heard it repeated on the river, from which we were not far distant. We repaired thither, and found two of the men, who had been left at the last ford, and who, having constructed a bark canoe, were descending the river. I made one of them disembark, and took his place, my knee being so painful that I could walk no further. Meanwhile the whole party came up; they loaded the horses, and pursued their route. In the course of the day my companion (an Iroquois) and I, shot seven ducks. Coming, at last, to a high promontory called *Millet's rock*, we found some of our foot-travellers with Messrs. Stewart and Clarke, who were on horseback, all at a stand, doubting whether it would answer to wade round the base of the rock, which dipped in the water. We sounded the stream for them, and found it fordable. So they all passed round, thereby avoiding the inland path, which is excessively fatiguing by reason of the hills, which it is necessary perpetually to mount and descend. We encamped, to the number of seven, at the entrance of what at high water might be a lake, but was then but a flat of blackish sand, with a narrow channel in the centre. Here we made an excellent supper on the wild ducks, while those who were behind had nothing to eat.

CHAPTER XXIV.

Arrival at the Fort of the Mountains.—Description of this Post.—Some Details in Regard to the Rocky Mountains.—Mountain Sheep, &c.—Continuation of the Journey.—Unhappy Accident.—Reflections.—News from Canada.—Hunter's Lodge.—Pimbina and Red Deer Rivers.

On the 19th we raised our camp and followed the shore of the little dry lake, along a smooth sandy beach, having abandoned our little bark canoe, both because it had become nearly unserviceable, and because we knew ourselves to be very near the Rocky Mountains House. In fact, we had not gone above five or six miles when we discerned a column of smoke on the opposite side of the stream. We immediately forded across, and arrived at the post, where we found Messrs. M'Donald, Stuart, and M'Kenzie, who had preceded us only two days.

The post of the Rocky Mountains, in English, *Rocky Mountains House*, is situated on the shore of the little lake I have mentioned, in the midst of a wood, and is surrounded, except on the water side, by steep rocks, inhabited only by the mountain sheep and goat. Here is seen in the west the chain of the Rocky Mountains, whose summits are covered with perpetual snow. On the lake side, *Millet's Rock*, of which I have spoken above, is in full view, of an immense height, and resembles the front of a huge church seen in perspective. The post was under the charge of a Mr. Decoigne. He does not procure many furs for the company, which has only established the house as a provision depôt, with the view of facilitating the passage of the mountains to those of its *employés* who are repairing to, or returning from, the Columbia.

People speak so often of the Rocky Mountains, and appear to know so little about them, that the reader will naturally desire me to say here a word on that subject. If we are to credit travellers, and the most recent maps, these mountains extend nearly in a straight line, from the 35th or 36th degree of north latitude, to the mouth of the *Unjighah*, or *M'Kenzie's river*, in the Arctic ocean, in latitude 65° or 66° N. This distance of thirty degrees of latitude, or seven hundred and fifty leagues, equivalent to two thousand two hundred and fifty English miles or thereabouts, is, however, only the mean side of a right-angled triangle, the base of which occupies twenty-six degrees of longitude, in latitude 35° or 36°, that is to say, is about sixteen hundred miles long, while the chain of mountains forms the *hypotenuse;* so that the real, and as it were diagonal, length of the chain, across the continent, must be very near three thousand miles from S. E. to N. W. In such a vast extent of mountains, the perpendicular height and width of base must necessarily be very unequal. We were about eight days in crossing them; whence I conclude, from our daily rate of travel, that they may have, at this point, i. e., about latitude 54°, a base of two hundred miles.

The geographer Pinkerton is assuredly mistaken, when he gives these mountains an elevation of but three thousand feet above the level of the sea; from my own observations I would not hesitate to give them six thousand; we attained, in crossing them, an elevation probably of fifteen hundred feet above the valleys, and were not, perhaps, nearer than half way of their total height, while the valleys themselves must be considerably elevated above the level of the Pacific, considering the prodigious number of rapids and falls which are met in the Columbia, from the first falls to Canoe river. Be that as it may, if these mountains yield to the Andes in elevation and extent, they very much surpass in both respects the Apalachian chain, regarded until recently as the principal mountains of North America: they give rise, accordingly, to an infinity of streams, and to the greatest rivers of the continent.*

* This is interesting, as the rough calculation of an unscientific traveller, unprovided with instruments, and at that date. The real height of the Rocky Mountains, as now ascertained, averages twelve thousand feet; the highest known peak is about sixteen thousand.—ED.

They offer a vast and unexplored field to natural history: no botanist, no mineralogist, has yet examined them. The first travellers called them the Glittering mountains, on account of the infinite number of immense rock crystals, which, they say, cover their surface, and which, when they are not covered with snow, or in the bare places, reflect to an immense distance the rays of the sun. The name of Rocky mountains was given them, probably, by later travellers, in consequence of the enormous isolated rocks which they offer here and there to the view. In fact, Millet's rock, and *Mc Gillivray's* above all, appeared to me wonders of nature. Some think that they contain metals, and precious stones.

With the exception of the mountain sheep and goat, the animals of the Rocky mountains, if these rocky passes support any, are not better known than their vegetable and mineral productions. The mountain sheep resorts generally to steep rocks, where it is impossible for men or even for wolves to reach them: we saw several on the rocks which surround the Mountain House.

This animal has great curved horns, like those of the domestic ram: its wool is long, but coarse; that on the belly is the finest and whitest. The Indians who dwell near the mountains, make blankets of it, similar to ours, which they exchange with the Indians of the Columbia for fish, and other commodities. The ibex, or mountain goat, frequents, like the sheep, the top and the declivities of the rocks: it differs from the sheep in having hair instead of wool, and straight horns projecting backward, instead of curved ones. The color is also different. The natives soften the horns of these animals by boiling, and make platters, spoons, &c., of them, in a very artistic manner.

Mr. Decoigne had not sufficient food for us, not having expected so many people to arrive at once. His hunters were then absent on *Smoke* river (so called by some travellers who saw in the neighborhood a volcanic mountain belching smoke), in quest of game. We were therefore compelled to kill one of the horses for food. We found no birch bark either to make canoes, and set the men to work in constructing some of wood. For want of better materials, we were obliged to use poplar. On the 22d, the three men whom we had left at the old-house, arrived in a little canoe made of two elk-skins sewed together, and stretched like a drum, on a frame of poles.

On the 24th, four canoes being ready, we fastened them together two and two, and embarked, to descend the river to an old post called *Hunter's Lodge*, where Mr. Decoigne, who was to return with us to Canada, informed us that we should find some bark canoes *en cache*, placed there for the use of the persons who descend the river. The water was not deep, and the stream was rapid; we glided along, so to speak, for ten or a dozen leagues, and encamped, having lost sight of the mountains. In proportion as we advanced, the banks of the river grew less steep, and the country became more agreeable.

On the 25th, having only a little *pemican* left, which we wished to keep, we sent forward a hunter in the little elk-skin canoe, to kill some game. About ten o'clock, we found him waiting for us with two moose that he had killed. He had suspended the hearts from the branch of a tree as a signal. We landed some men to help him in cutting up and shipping the game. We continued to glide safely down. But toward two o'clock, P. M., after doubling a point, we got into a considerable rapid, where, by the maladroitness of those who managed the double pirogue in which I was, we met with a melancholy accident. I had proposed to go ashore, in order to lighten the canoes, which were loaded to the water's edge; but the steersman insisted that we could go down safe, while the bow-man was turning the head of the pirogue toward the beach; by this manœuvre we were brought athwart the stream, which was carrying us fast toward the falls; just then our frail bark struck upon a sunken rock; the lower canoe broke amid-ships and filled instantly, and the upper one being lighted, rolled over, precipitating us all into the water. Two of our men, Olivier Roy Lapensée and André Bélanger, were drowned;

and it was not without extreme difficulty that we succeeded in saving Messrs. Pillet and Wallace, as well as a man named *J. Hurteau.* The latter was so far gone that we were obliged to have recourse to the usual means for the resuscitation of drowned persons. The men lost all their effects; the others recovered but a part of theirs; and all our provisions went. Toward evening, in ascending the river (for I had gone about two miles below, to recover the effects floating down), we found the body of Lapensée. We interred it as decently as we could, and planted at his grave a cross, on which I inscribed with the point of my knife, his name and the manner and date of his death. Bélanger's body was not found. If anything could console the shades of the departed for a premature and unfortunate end, it would be, no doubt, that the funeral rites have been paid to their remains, and that they themselves have given their names to the places where they perished: it is thus that the shade of Palinurus rejoiced in the regions below, at learning from the mouth of the Sibyl, that the promontory near which he was drowned would henceforth be called by his name: *gaudet cognomine terra.* The rapid and the point of land where the accident I have described took place, will bear, and bears already, probably, the name of *Lapensée*.*

On the 26th, a part of our people embarked in the three canoes which remained, and the others followed the banks of the river on foot. We saw in several places some veins of bituminous coal, on the banks between the surface of the water and that of the plain, say thirty feet below the latter; the veins had a dip of about 25°. We tried some and found it to burn well. We halted in the evening near a small stream, where we constructed some rafts, to carry all our people.

On the 27th, I went forward in the little canoe

* Mr. Franchere, not having the fear of the *Abbé Gaume* before his eyes, so wrote in his Journal of 1814; finding consolation in a thought savoring, we confess, more of Virgil than of the catechism. It is a classic term that calls to our mind rough Captain *Thorn's* sailor-like contempt for his literary passengers so comically described by Mr. *Irving*. Half of the humor as well as of the real interest of Mr. Franchere's charming narrative, is lost by one who has never read "Astoria."

of skins, with the two hunters. We soon killed an elk, which we skinned and suspended the hide, besmeared with blood, from the branch of a tree at the extremity of a point, in order that the people behind, as they came up, might perceive and take in the fruit of our chase. After fortifying ourselves with a little food, we continued to glide down, and encamped for the night near a thick wood where our hunters, from the tracks they observed, had hopes of encountering and capturing some bears. This hope was not realized.

On the 28th, a little after quitting camp, we killed a swan. While I was busy cooking it, the hunters having plunged into the wood, I heard a rifle-shot, which seemed to me to proceed from a direction opposite to that which they had taken. They returned very soon running, and were extremely surprised to learn that it was not I who had fired it. Nevertheless, the canoes and rafts having overtaken us, we continued to descend the river. Very soon we met a bark canoe, containing two men and a woman, who were ascending the river and bringing letters and some goods for the *Rocky Mountains House*. We learned from these letters addressed to Mr. Decoigne, several circumstances of the war, and among others the defeat of Captain Barclay on Lake Erie. We arrived that evening at *Hunter's Lodge*, where we found four new birch-bark canoes. We got ready two of them, and resumed our journey down, on the 31st. Mr. Pillet set out before us with the hunters, at a very early hour. They killed an elk, which they left on a point, and which we took in. The country through which we passed that day is the most charming possible; the river is wide, handsome, and bordered with low outjutting points, covered with birch and poplar.

On the 1st of June, in the evening, we encamped at the confluence of the river *Pembina*. This stream comes from the south, and takes its rise in one of the spurs of the great chain of the Rocky mountains; ascending it for two days, and crossing a neck of land about seventy-five miles, one reaches Fort Augustus, a trading post on the *Saskatchawine* river. Messrs. M'Donald and M'Kenzie had taken this route, and had left for us half a sack of pemican in a *cache*, at the mouth of the river *Pembina*. After landing that evening, Mr. Stuart and I amused ourselves with angling, but took only five or six small fish.

On the 2d, we passed the confluence of *Little Slave Lake* river. At eight o'clock in the morning, we met a band or family of Indians, of the *Knisteneaux* tribe. They had just killed a buffalo, which we bought of them for a small brass-kettle. We could not have had a more seasonable *rencontre*, for our provisions were all consumed.

On the 3d, we reached *Little Red Elk* river, which we began to ascend, quitting the *Athabasca*, or *Great Red Elk*. This stream was very narrow in its channel, and obstructed with boulders: we were obliged to take to the shore, while some of the men dragged along the canoes. Their method was to lash poles across, and wading themselves, lift the canoes over the rocks—a laborious and infinitely tedious operation. The march along the banks was not less disagreeable: for we had to traverse points of forest where the fire had passed, and which were filled with fallen trees.

Wallace and I having stopped to quench our thirst at a rill, the rest got in advance of us; and we lost our way in a labyrinth of buffalo tracks which we mistook for the trail, so that we wandered about for three hours before we came up with the party, who began to fear for our safety, and were firing signal-guns to direct us. As the river now grew deeper, we all embarked in the canoes, and about evening overtook our hunters, who had killed a moose and her two calves.

We continued our journey on the 4th, sometimes seated in our canoes, sometimes marching along the river on foot, and encamped in the evening, excessively fatigued.

CHAPTER XXV.

Red Deer Lake.—Antoine Déjarlais.—Beaver River.—N. Nadeau.—Moose River.—Bridge Lake.—Saskatchawine River.—Fort Vermilion.—Mr. Hallet.—Trading-Houses.—Beautiful Country.—Reflections.

THE 5th of June brought us to the beautiful sheet of water called *Red Deer lake*, irregular in shape, dotted with islands, and about forty miles in length by thirty in its greatest width. We met, about the middle of it, a small canoe conducted by two young women. They were searching for gulls' and ducks' eggs on the islands, this being the season of laying for those aquatics. They told us that their father was not far distant from the place where we met them. In fact, we presently saw him appear in a canoe with his two boys, rounding a little isle. We joined him, and learned that his name was

Antoine Déjarlais; that he had been a guide in the service of the Northwest Company, but had left them since 1805. On being made acquainted with our need of provisions, he offered us a great quantity of eggs, and made one of our men embark with his two daughters in their little canoe, to seek some more substantial supplies at his cabin, on the other side of the lake. He himself accompanied us as far as a portage of about twenty-five yards formed at the outlet of the lake by a Beaver dam. Having performed the portage, and passed a small pond or marsh, we encamped to await the return of our man. He arrived the next morning, with Déjarlais, bringing us about fifty pounds of dried venison and from ten to twelve pounds of tallow. We invited our host to breakfast with us: it was the least we could do after the good offices he had rendered us. This man was married to an Indian woman, and lived with his family, on the produce of his chase; he appeared quite contented with his lot. Nobody at least disputed with him the sovereignty of Red-Deer lake, of which he had, as it were, taken possession. He begged me to read for him two letters which he had had in his possession for two years, and of which he did not yet know the contents. They were from one of his sisters, and dated at *Verchères*, in Canada. I even thought that I recognised the handwriting of Mr. L. G. Labadie, teacher of that parish. At last, having testified to this good man, in suitable terms, our gratitude for the services he had rendered us, we quitted him and prosecuted our journey.

After making two portages, we arrived on the banks of Beaver river, which was here but a rivulet. It is by this route that the canoes ordinarily pass to reach Little Slave lake and the Athabasca country, from the head of Lake Superior, via., *Cumberland House*, on *English river*. We were obliged by the shallowness of the stream, to drag along our canoes, walking on a bottom or beach of sand, where we began to feel the importunity of the mosquitoes. One of the hunters scoured the woods for game but without success. By-and-by we passed a small canoe turned bottom up and covered with a blanket. Soon after we came to a cabin or lodge, where we found an old Canadian hunter named *Nadeau*. He was reduced to the last stage of weakness, having had nothing to eat for two days. Nevertheless, a young man who was married to one of his daughters, came in shortly after, with the good news that he had just killed a buffalo; a circumstance which determined us to encamp there for the night. We sent some of our men to get in the meat. Nadeau gave us half of it, and told us that we should find, thirty miles lower down, at the foot of a pine tree, a *cache*, where he had deposited ten swan-skins, and some of martin, with a net, which he prayed us to take to the next trading-post. We quitted this good fellow the next morning, and pursued our way. Arriving at the place indicated, we found the *cache*, and took the net, leaving the other articles. A short distance further, we came to Moose river, which we had to ascend, in order to reach the lake of that name. The water in this river was so low that we were obliged entirely to unload the canoes, and to lash poles across them, as we had done before, that the men might carry them on their shoulders over the places where they could not be floated. Having distributed the baggage to the remainder of the hands, we pursued our way through the woods, under the guidance of Mr. Decoigne.

This gentleman, who had not passed here for nineteen years, soon lost his way, and we got separated into small parties, in the course of the afternoon, some going one way, and some another, in search of Moose lake. But as we had outstripped the men who carried the baggage and the small stock of provision that old Nadeau had given us, Mr. Wallace and I thought it prudent to retrace our steps and keep with the rear-guard. We soon met Mr. Pillet and one of the hunters. The latter, ferreting the woods on both sides of a trail that he had discovered, soon gave a whoop, to signify that we should stop. Presently emerging from the underwood, he showed us a horsewhip which he had found, and from which and from other unmistakeable signs, he was confident the trail would lead either to the lake or a navigable part of the river. The men with the baggage then coming up, we entered the thicket single file, and were conducted by this path, in a very short time, to the river, on the banks of which were visible the traces of an old camping ground. The night was coming on; and soon after, the canoes arrived, to our great satisfaction; for we had begun to fear that they had already passed. The splashing of their paddles was a welcome sound, and we who had been wise enough to keep behind, all encamped together.

Very early on the 8th, I set out accompanied by one of the hunters, in quest of Messrs. D. Stuart, Clarke and Decoigne, who had gone on ahead, the night previons. I soon found MM. Clarke and M'Gillis encamped on the shore of the lake. The canoes presently arrived and we embarked; MM. Stuart and Decoigne rejoined us shortly after, and informed us that they had bivouacked on the shore of Lac *Puant*, or Stinking lake, a pond situated about twelve miles E. N. E. from the lake we were now entering.

Finding ourselves thus reunited, we traversed the latter, which is about eighteen miles in circuit, and has very pretty shores. We encamped, very early, on an island, in order to use old Nadeau's fishing net. I visited it that evening and brought back three carp and two water-hens. We left it set all night, and the next morning found in it twenty white-fish. Leaving camp at an early hour, we gained the entrance of a small stream that descends between some hills of moderate elevation, and there stopped to breakfast. I found the white-fish more delicious in flavor, even than the salmon. We had again to foot it, following the bank of this little stream. It was a painful task, as we were obliged to open a path through thick underbrush, in the midst of a rain that lasted all day and kept us drenched. Two men being left in each canoe, conveyed them up the river about thirty miles, as far as Long lake—a narrow pond, on the margin of which we spent the night.

On the 10th, we got through this lakelet, and entered another small stream, which it was necessary to navigate in the same manner as the preceding, and which conducted us to Bridge lake. The latter received its name from a sort of bridge or causeway, formed at its southern extremity, and which is nothing more than a huge beaver dam. We found here a lodge, where were a young man and two women, who had charge of some horses appertaining to one of the Hudson's Bay trading houses. We borrowed of them half a dozen pack horses, and crossed the bridge with them. After surmounting a considerable hill, we reached an open, level, and dry prairie, which conducted us in about two hours to an ancient trading-post on the banks of the *Saskatchawine*. Knowing that we were near a factory, we made our toilets as well as we could, before arriving. Toward sundown, we reached Fort Vermilion, which is situated on the bank of a river, at the foot of a superb hill.

We found at this post some ninety persons, men, women, and children; these people depend for subsistence on the chase, and fishing with hooks and lines, which is very precarious. Mr. Hallet, the clerk in charge was absent, and we were dismayed to hear that there were no provisions on the place: a very disagreeable piece of news for people famished as we were. We had been led to suppose that if we could only reach the plains of the Saskatchawine, we should be in the land of plenty. Mr. Hallet, however, was not long in arriving: he had two quarters of buffalo meat brought out, which had been laid in ice, and prepared us supper. Mr. Hallet was a polite sociable man, loving his ease passably well, and desirous of living in these wild countries, as people do in civilized lands. Having testified to him our surprise at seeing in one of the buildings a large *cariole*, like those of Canada, he informed us that having horses, he had had this carriage made in order to enjoy a sleigh-ride; but that the workmen having forgot to take the measure of the doors of the building before constructing it, it was found when finished, much too large for them, and could never be got out of the room where it was; and it was like to remain there a long time, as he was not disposed to demolish the house for the pleasure of using the cariole.

By the side of the factory of the Northwest Company, is another belonging to the Company of Hudson's Bay. In general these trading-houses are constructed thus, one close to the other, and surrounded with a common palisade, with a door of communication in the interior for mutual succor, in case of attack on the part of the Indians. The latter, in this region, particularly the Black-feet, *Gros-ventres*, and those of the Yellow river, are very ferocious: they live by the chase, but bring few furs to the traders; and the latter maintain these posts principally to procure themselves provisions.

On the 11th, after breakfasting at Fort Vermilion, we resumed our journey, with six or seven pounds of tallow for our whole stock of food. This slender supply brought us through to the evening of the third day, when we had for supper two ounces of tallow each.

On the 14th, in the morning, we killed a wild

goose, and toward midday, collected some flag-root and *choux-gras*, a wild herb, which we boiled with the small game: we did not forget to throw into the pot the little tallow we had left, and made a delicious repast. Toward the decline of day, we had the good luck to kill a buffalo.

On the 15th, MM. Clarke and Decoigne having landed during our course, to hunt, returned presently with the agreeable intelligence that they had killed three buffaloes. We immediately encamped, and sent the greater part of the men to cut up the meat and jerk it. This operation lasted till the next evening, and we set forward again in the canoes on the 17th, with about six hundred pounds of meat half cured. The same evening we perceived from our camp several herds of buffaloes, but did not give chase, thinking we had enough meat to take us to the next post.

The river *Saskatchawine* flows over a bed composed of sand and marl, which contributes not a little to diminish the purity and transparency of its waters, which, like those of the Missouri, are turbid and whitish. Except for that it is one of the prettiest rivers in the world. The banks are perfectly charming, and offer in many places a scene the fairest, the most smiling, and the best diversified that can be seen or imagined: hills in varied forms, crowned with superb groves; valleys agreeably embrowned, at evening and morning, by the prolonged shadow of the hills, and of the woods which adorn them; herds of light-limbed antelopes, and heavy colossal buffalo—the former bounding along the slopes of the hills, the latter trampling under their heavy feet the verdure of the plains; all these champaign beauties reflected and doubled as it were, by the waters of the river; the melodious and varied song of a thousand birds, perched on the tree-tops; the refreshing breath of the zephyrs; the serenity of the sky; the purity and salubrity of the air; all, in a word, pours contentment and joy into the soul of the enchanted spectator. It is above all in the morning, when the sun is rising, and in the evening when he is setting, that the spectacle is really ravishing. I could not detach my regards from that superb picture, till the nascent obscurity had obliterated its perfection. Then, to the sweet pleasure that I had tasted, succeeded a *triste*, not to say, a sombre, melancholy. How comes it to pass, I said to myself, that so beautiful a country is not inhabited by human creatures? The songs, the hymns, the prayers, of the laborer and the artisan, shall they never be heard in these fine plains? Wherefore, while in Europe, and above all in England, so many thousands of men do not possess as their own an inch of ground, and cultivate the soil of their country for proprietors who scarcely leave them whereon to support existence;—wherefore—do so many millions of acres of apparently fat and fertile land, remain uncultivated and absolutely useless? Or, at least, why do they support only herds of wild animals? Will men always love better to vegetate all their lives on an ungrateful soil, than to seek afar fertile regions, in order to pass in peace and plenty, at least the last portion of their days? But I deceive myself; it is not so easy as one thinks, for the poor man to better his condition: he has not the means of transporting himself to distant countries, or he has not those of acquiring a property there; for these untilled lands, deserted, abandoned, do not appertain to whoever wishes to establish himself upon them and reduce them to culture; they have owners, and from these must be purchased the right of rendering them productive! Besides one ought not to give way to illusions: these countries, at times so delightful, do not enjoy a perpetual spring; they have their winter, and a rigorous one; a piercing cold is then spread through the atmosphere; deep snows cover the surface; the frozen rivers flow only for the fish; the trees are stripped of their leaves and hung with icicles; the verdure of the plains has disappeared; the hills and valleys offer but a uniform whiteness; Nature has lost all her beauty; and man has enough to do, to shelter himself from the injuries of the inclement season.

CHAPTER XXVI.

Fort Montée.—Cumberland House.—Lake Bourbon.—Great Winipeg Rapids.—Lake Winipeg.—Trading-House.—Lake of the Woods.—Rainy Lake House, &c.

On the 18th of June (a day which its next anniversary was to render for ever celebrated in the annals of the world), we re-embarked at an early hour: and the wind rising, spread sail, a thing we had not done before, since we quitted the river Columbia. In the afternoon the clouds gathered thick and black, and we had a gust, accompanied with hail, but of short duration; the weather cleared up again, and about sundown we arrived at *Le Fort de la Montée*, so called, on account of its being a depôt, where the traders going south, leave their canoes and take pack-horses to reach their several posts. We found here, as at Fort Vermilion, two trading-houses joined together, to make common cause against the Indians; one belonging to the Hudson's Bay Company, the other to the company of the Northwest: the Hudson's Bay house being then under the charge of a Mr. Prudent, and the N. W. Company's under a Mr. John M'Lean. Mr. de Roche Blave, one of the partners of the last company having the superintendence of this district, where he had wintered, had gone to Lake Superior to attend the annual meeting of the partners. There were cultivated fields around the house; the barley and peas appeared to promise an abundant harvest. Mr. M'Lean received us as well as circumstances permitted; but that gentleman having no food to give us, and our buffalo meat beginning to spoil, we set off the next morning, to reach Cumberland house as quick as possible. In the course of the day, we passed two old forts, one of which had been built by the French before the conquest of Canada. According to our guide, it was the most distant western post that the French traders ever had in the northwestern wilderness. Toward evening we shot a moose. The aspect of the country changes considerably since leaving *Montée;* the banks of the river rise more boldly, and the country is covered with forests.

On the 20th, we saw some elms—a tree that I had not seen hitherto, since my departure from Canada. We reached Fort Cumberland a little before the setting of the sun. This post, called in English *Cumberland House*, is situated at the outlet of the *Saskatchawine*, where it empties into *English lake*, between the 53d and 54th degrees of north latitude. It is a depot for those traders who are going to Slave lake or the Athabasca, or are returning thence, as well as for those destined for the Rocky mountains. It was under the orders of Mr. J. D. Campbell, who having gone down to Fort William, however, had left it in charge of a Mr. Harrison. There are two factories, as at Vermilion and la Montée. At this place the traders who resort every year to Fort William, leave their half-breed or Indian wives and families, as they can live here at little expense, the lake abounding in fish. Messrs.

Clarke and Stuart, who were behind, arrived on the 22d, and in the evening we had a dance. They gave us four sacs of pemican, and we set off again, on the 23d, at eight A. M. Wé crossed the lake, and entered a small river, and having made some eighty or ninety miles under sail, encamped on a low shore, where the mosquitoes tormented us horribly all night.

On the 24th, we passed *Muddy* lake, and entered Lake *Bourbon*, where we fell in with a canoe from *York* factory, under the command of a Mr. Kennedy, clerk of the Hudson's Bay Company. We collected some dozens of gulls' eggs, on the rocky islands of the lake: and stopping on one of the last at night, having a little flour left, Mr. Decoigne and I amused ourselves in making fritters for the next day's breakfast: an occupation, which despite the small amount of materials, employed us till we were surprised by the daybreak; the night being but brief at this season in that high latitude.

At sunrise on the 25th, we were again afloat, passed Lake *Travers*, or *Cross* lake, which empties into Lake Winipeg by a succession of rapids; shot down these cascades without accident, and arrived, toward noon, at the great rapid *Ouénipic* or Winipeg, which is about four miles long. We disembarked here, and the men worked down the canoes. At the foot of this rapid, which is the inlet of Winipeg, we found an old Canadian fisherman, who called himself *King of the lake.* He might fairly style himself king of the fish, which are abundant and which he alone enjoyed. Having made a boil, and regaled ourselves with excellent sturgeon, we left this old man, and entered the great lake Winipeg, which appeared to me like a sea of fresh water. This lake is now too well known to need a particular description: I will content myself with saying that it visibly yields in extent only to Lake Superior and Great Slave lake: it has for tributaries several large rivers, and among others the Saskatchawine, the Winipeg, in the east; and Red river in the south; and empties into Hudson's bay by the *Nelson*, N. N. E., and the *Severn*, E. N. E. The shores which it bathes are generally very low; it appears to have little depth, and is dotted with a vast number of islands, lying pretty close to land. We reached one called *Egg island*, whence it was necessary to cross to the south to reach the main; but the wind was so violent that it was only at decline of day that we could perform the passage. We profited by the calm, to coast along all day and a part of the night of the 26th; but to pay for it, remained in camp on the 27th, till evening: the wind not suffering us to proceed. The wind having appeared to abate somewhat after sunset, we embarked, but were soon forced to land again. On the 28th, we passed the openings of several deep bays, and the isles of *St. Martin*, and camped at the bottom of a little bay, where the mosquitoes did not suffer us to close our eyes all night. We were rejoiced when dawn appeared, and were eager to embark, to free ourselves from these inconvenient guests. A calm permitted us that day to make good progress with our oars, and we camped at *Buffalo Strait*. We saw that day two Indian wigwams.

The 30th brought us to Winipeg river, which we began to ascend, and about noon reached Fort *Bas de la Rivière*. This trading post had more the air of a large and well-cultivated farm, than of a fur traders' factory: a neat and elegant mansion, built on a slight eminence, and surrounded with barns, stables, storehouses, &c., and by fields of barley, peas, oats, and potatoes, reminded us of the civilized countries which we had left so long ago. Messrs. Crébassa and Kennedy, who had this post in charge, received us with all possible hospitality, and supplied us with all the political news which had been learned through the arrival of canoes from Canada.

They also informed us that Messrs M'Donald and de Rocheblave had passed, a few days before our arrival, having been obliged to go up Red river to stop the effusion of blood, which would probably have taken place but for their intervention, in the colony founded on that river by the earl of Selkirk. Mr. Miles M'Donnell, the governor of that colony, or rather of the *Assiniboyne* district, had issued a proclamation forbidding all persons whomsoever, to send provisions of any kind out of the district. The Hudson's Bay traders had conformed to this proclamation, but those of the Northwest Company paid no attention to it, thinking it illegal, and had sent their servants, as usual to get provisions up the river. Mr. M'Donnell having heard that several hundred sacks of pemican* were laid up in a storehouse under the care of a Mr. Pritchard, sent to require their surrender: Pritchard refused to deliver them, whereupon Mr. M'Donnell had them carried off by force. The traders who winter on Little Slave lake, English river, the Athabasca country, &c., learning this, and being aware that they would not

* *Pemican*, of which I have already spoken several times, is the Indian name for the dried and pounded meat which the natives sell to the traders. About fifty pounds of this meat is placed in a trough (*un grand vaisseau fait d'un tronc d'arbre*), and about an equal quantity of tallow is melted and poured over it; it is thoroughly mixed into one mass, and when cold, is put up in bags made of undressed buffalo hide, with the hair outside, and sewed up as tightly as possible. The meat thus impregnated with tallow, hardens, and will keep for years. It is eaten without any other preparation; but sometimes wild pears or dried berries are added, which render the flavor more agreeable.

find their usual supply at *Bas de la Rivière*, resolved to go and recover the seized provisions by force, if they were not peaceably given up. Things were in this position when Messrs. de Rocheblave and M'Donald arrived. They found the Canadian *voyageurs* in arms, and ready to give battle to the colonists, who persisted in their refusal to surrender the bags of pemican. The two peacemakers visited the governor, and having explained to him the situation in which the traders of the Northwest Company would find themselves, by the want of necessary provisions to enable them to transport their peltries to Fort William, and the exasperation of their men, who saw no other alternative for them, but to get possession of those provisions or to perish of hunger, requested him to surrender the same without delay. Mr. M'Donnell, on his part, pointed out the misery to which the colonists would be reduced by a failure in the supply of food. In consequence of these mutual representations, it was agreed that one half of the pemican should be restored, and the other half remain for the use of the colonists. Thus was arranged, without bloodshed, the first difficulty which occurred between the rival companies of the Northwest, and of Hudson's Bay.

Having spent the 1st of July in repairing our canoes, we re-embarked on the 2d, and continued to ascend Winipeg river, called also *White river*, on account of the great number of its cascades, which being very near each other, offer to the sight an almost continuous foam. We made that day twenty-seven portages, all very short. On the 3d, and 4th, we made nine more, and arrived on the 5th, at the *Lake of the Woods*. This lake takes its name from the great number of woody islands with which it is dotted. Our guide pointed out to me one of these isles, telling me that a Jesuit father had said mass there, and that it was the most remote spot to which those missionaries had ever penetrated. We encamped on one of the islands. The next day the wind did not allow us to make much progress. On the 7th, we gained the entrance of *Rainy Lake river*. I do not remember ever to have seen elsewhere so many mosquitoes as on the banks of this river. Having landed near a little rapid to lighten the canoes, we had the misfortune, in getting through the brush, to dislodge these insects from under the leaves where they had taken refuge from the rain of the night before; they attached themselves to us, followed us into the canoes, and tormented us all the remainder of the day.

On the 8th, at sunset, we reached *Rainy Lake House*. This fort is situated about a mile from a considerable rapid. We saw here cultivated fields and domestic animals, such as horses, oxen, cows, &c. The port is a depôt for the wintering parties of the Athabasca, and others still more remote, who bring to it their peltries and return from it with their outfits of merchandise. Mr. John Dease, to whose charge the place had been confided, received us in the most friendly manner possible; and after having made an excellent supper, we danced a part of the evening.

We took leave of Mr. Dease on the 10th, well provided for the journey, and passing round

Rainy Lake falls, and then traversing the lake itself, which I estimated to be forty miles long, we encamped at the entrance of a small river. On the next day we pursued our way, now thridding streams impeded with wild rice, which rendered our progress difficult, now traversing little lakes, now passing straits where we scarcely found water to float our canoes. On the 13th, we encamped near *Dog Portage* (*Portage des chiens*), where, from not having followed the advice of Mr. Dease, who had counselled us to take along a bag of pemican, we found ourselves absolutely without food.

CHAPTER XXVII.

Arrival at Fort William.—Description of the Fort.—News from the River Columbia.

STARVING men are early-risers. We set out on the 14th before day, and effected the portage, which is long and difficult. At the foot of the rapid we found a sort of *restaurant* or *cabaret*, kept by a man named *Boucher*. We treated the men to a little *eau de vie*, and breakfasted on some detestable sausages, poisoned with salt.

After this wretched repast, we set out again, and passed toward noon, the *Mountain Portage*. Here the river *Kaministiquia* flings itself over a rock of immense height, and forms a fall scarcely less curious to see than that of Niagara. Below, the succession of falls and rapids is constant, so that we made no fewer than thirty-six portages in the course of the day. Nevertheless we pursued our laborious way with good cheer, and without a murmur from our Canadian boatmen, who kept their spirits up by singing their *voyageur* songs. At last, at about nine o'clock in the evening, we arrived at Fort William.

Fort William is situated on Lake Superior, at the mouth of the *Kaministiquia* river, about forty-five miles north of old *Grand Portage.* It was built in 1805, when the two rival Canadian companies were united, and was named in honor of Mr. (now the Honorable) William M'Gillivray, principal agent of the Northwest Company. The proprietors, perceiving that the old fort of *Grand Portage* was on the territory claimed by the American government, resolved to demolish it and build another on the British territory. No site appeared more advantageous than the present for the purposes intended; the river is deep, of easy access, and offers a safe harbor for shipping. It is true they had to contend with all the difficulties consequent on a low and swampy soil; but by incredible labor and perseverance they succeeded in draining the marshes and reducing the loose and yielding soil to solidity.

Fort William has really the appearance of a fort, with its palisade fifteen feet high, and that of a pretty village, from the number of edifices it encloses. In the middle of a spacious square rises a large building elegantly constructed, though of wood, with a long piazza or portico, raised about five feet from the ground, and surmounted by a balcony, extending along the whole front. In the centre is a saloon or hall, sixty feet in length by thirty in width, decorated with several pieces of painting, and some portraits of the leading partners. It is in this hall that the agents, partners, clerks, interpreters, and guides, take their meals together, at different tables. At each extremity of the apartment are two rooms; two of these are destined for the two principal agents; the other two to the steward and his department. The kitchen and servants' rooms are in the basement. On either side of this edifice, is another of the same extent, but of less elevation; they are each divided by a corridor running through its length, and contain each, a dozen pretty bed-rooms. One is destined for the wintering partners, the other for the clerks. On the east of the square is another building similar to the last two, and intended for the same use, and a warehouse where the furs are inspected and repacked for shipment. In the rear of these, are the lodging-house of the guides, another fur-warehouse, and finally, a powder magazine. The last is of stone, and has a roof covered with tin. At the angle is a sort of bastion, or look-out place, commanding a view of the lake. On the west side is seen a range of buildings, some of which serve for stores, and others for workshops; there is one for the equipment of the men, another for the fitting out of the canoes, one for the retail of goods, another where they sell liquors, bread, pork, butter, &c., and where a treat is given to the travellers who arrive. This consists in a white loaf, half a pound of butter, and a gill of rum. The *voyageurs* give this tavern the name of *Cantine salope*. Behind all this is another range, where we find the counting-house, a fine square building, and well-lighted ; another storehouse of stone, tin-roofed ; and a *jail*, not less necessary than the rest. The *voyageurs* give it the name of *pot au beurre*—the butter-tub. Beyond these we discover the shops of the carpenter, the cooper, the tinsmith, the blacksmith, &c. ; and spacious yards and sheds for the shelter, reparation, and construction of canoes. Near the gate of the fort, which is on the south, are the quarters of the physician, and those of the chief clerk. Over the gate is a guard-house.

As the river is deep at its entrance, the company has had a wharf constructed, extending the whole length of the fort, for the discharge of the vessels which it keeps on Lake Superior, whether to transport its furs from Fort William to the *Saut Ste. Marie*, or merchandise and provisions from *Saut Ste. Marie* to Fort William. The land behind the fort and on both sides of it, is cleared and under tillage. We saw barley, peas, and oats, which had a very fine appearance. At the end of the clearing is the burying-ground. There are also, on the opposite bank of the river, a certain number of log-houses, all inhabited by old Canadian *voyageurs*, worn out in the service of the company, without having enriched themselves. Married to women of the country, and incumbered with large families of half-breed children, these men prefer to cultivate a little Indian corn and potatoes, and to fish, for a subsistence, rather than return to their native districts, to give their relatives and former acquaintance certain proofs of their misconduct or their imprudence.

Fort William is the grand depôt of the Northwest Company for their interior posts, and the general *rendezvous* of the partners. The agents from Montreal and the wintering partners assemble here every summer, to receive the returns of the respective outfits, prepare for the operations of the ensuing season, and discuss the general interests of their association. The greater part of them were assembled at the time of our arrival. The wintering hands who are to return with their employers, pass also a great part of the summer here; they form a great encampment on the west side of the fort, outside the palisades. Those who engage at Montreal to go no further than Fort William or *Rainy lake*, and who do not *winter*, occupy yet another space, on the east side. The winterers, or *hivernants*, give to these last the name of *mangeurs de lard*, or pork-eaters. They are also called *comers-and-goers*. One perceives an astonishing difference between these two camps, which are composed sometimes of three or four hundred men each; that of the pork-eaters is always dirty and disorderly, while that of the winterers is clean and neat.

To clear its land and improve its property, the company inserts a clause in the engagement of all who enter its service as canoe-men, that they shall work for a certain number of days during their stay at Fort William. It is thus that it has cleared and drained the environs of the fort, and has erected so many fine buildings. But when a hand has once worked the stipulated number of days, he is for ever after exempt, even if he remain in the service twenty or thirty years, and should come down to the fort every summer.

They received us very courteously at Fort William, and I perceived by the reception given to myself in particular, that thanks to the Chinook dialect of which I was sufficiently master, they would not have asked better than to give me employment, on advantageous terms. But I felt a great deal more eagerness to arrive in Montreal, than desire to return to the River Columbia.

A few days after we reached Fort William, Mr. Keith made his appearance there from Fort George, or Astoria, with the news of the arrival of the "Isaac Todd" in the Columbia river. This vessel, which was a dull sailer, had been kept back a long time by contrary winds in doubling Cape Horn, and had never been able to rejoin the vessels-of-war, her consorts, from which she was then separated. When she reached the *rendezvous* at the island of Juan Fernandez, finding that the three ships-of-war had sailed, the captain and passengers, as they were short of provisions, determined to range the coast. Entering the harbor of *Monterey*,* on the coast of California, in order to obtain provisions, they learned that there was an English vessel-of-war in distress, in the bay of *San Francisco*.† They repaired thither accordingly, and found, to their great surprise, that it was the sloop *Raccoon*. This vessel, in getting out of the River Columbia, had touched on the bar, with such violence, that a part of her false keel was carried away; and she had with difficulty made San Francisco, with seven feet of water in the hold, although her crew had been constantly at the pumps. Captain Black, finding it impossible to repair his ship, had decided to abandon her, and to cross the continent to the Gulf of Mexico, thence to reach some of the British West India islands. However, on the arrival of the Isaac Todd,

* A Spanish mission or presidency, in about the 36th degree of latitude.

† Another Spanish presidency, in about the 38th degree of latitude, and the first European establishment to be met with south of the Columbia. [These now obsolete notes are interesting as indicative of the period when they were written.—Ed.]

means were found to careen the vessel and repair the damage. The Isaac Todd then pursued her voyage and entered the Columbia on the 17th of April, thirteen months after her departure from England.

CHAPTER XXVIII.

Departure from Fort William.—Navigation on Lake Superior.—Michipicoton Bay.—Meeting a Canoe.—Batchawainon Bay.—Arrival at Saut Ste Marie.—Occurrences there.—Departure.—Lake Huron.—French River.—Lake Nipissing.—Ottawa River.—Kettle Falls.—Rideau River.—Long-Saut.—Arrival in Montreal.—Conclusion.

On the 20th of July, in the evening, Mr. D. Stuart notified me that he should start the next morning for Montreal, in a light canoe. I immediately wrote to my relatives: but the next morning Mr. Stuart told me that I was to be myself the bearer of my letters, by embarking with him. I got ready my effects, and toward evening we quitted Fort William, with fourteen stout *voyageurs* to man our large canoe, and were soon floating on the bosom of the largest body of fresh water on the surface of the globe. We counted six passengers, namely, Messrs. D.

Stuart, D. M'Kenzie, J. M'Donald, J. Clarke, myself, and a little girl of eight or nine years, who came from Kildonan, on Red river. We passed the first night on one of the islands in *Thunder bay*, so named on account of the frequent storms, accompanied with lightning and thunder, which burst over it at certain seasons of the year. On the 22d and 23d, we continued to range the southern coast of Lake Superior. The navigation of this superb lake would be extremely agreeable but for the thick fogs which reign during a part of the day, and do not permit a rapid progress. On the 24th, we dined at a small trading establishment called *Le Pic*, where we had excellent fish.

On the 26th, we crossed *Michipicoton bay*, which, at its entrance, may be nine miles wide, and twenty fathoms deep. As we were nearing the eastern point, we met a small canoe, having on board Captain M'Cargo, and the crew of one of the schooners owned by the company. Mr. M'Cargo informed us that he had just escaped from *Saut Ste. Marie*, whither the Americans had sent a detachment of one hundred and fifty men; and that having been obliged to abandon his schooner, he had set fire to her. In consequence of this news it was resolved that the canoe on which we were proceeding, should return to Fort William. I embarked, with Mr. Stuart and two men, in Captain M'Cargo's canoe, while he and his crew took our places. In the haste and confusion of this exchange, which was made on the lake, they gave us a ham, a little tea and sugar, and a bag containing about twenty-five pounds of flour, but forgot entirely a kettle, knives, forks, and so on, all articles which Mr. M'Cargo had not time to take when he left *Saut Ste. Marie.* We subsisted miserably in consequence for two days and a half that we continued to coast the lake before reaching any post. We moistened in the bag a little flour, and having kneaded it, made cakes, which we baked on flat stones by our camp fire.

On the 29th, we reached Batchawainon, where we found some women, who prepared us food and received us well. It is a poor little post, situated at the bottom of a sandy cove, which offers nothing agreeable to the eye. Mr. Frederic Goedike, who resided here, was gone to see what had taken place at Saut Ste. Marie. He returned the next day, and told us that the Americans had come, with a force of one hundred and fifty men, under the command of Major Holmes; and that after having pillaged that they all considered worth taking, of the property of the N. W. Company and that of a Mr. Johnston, they had set fire to the houses, warehouses, &c., belonging to the company and to that gentleman, and retired, without molesting any other person.* Our canoe arrived from Fort William in the evening, with that of Mr. M'Gillivray; and on the morrow we all repaired to Saut Ste. Marie, where we saw the ruins which the enemy had left. The houses, stores, and saw-mills of the company were still smoking.

* The N. W. Company having raised a regiment composed of their own servants, and known as the *voyageur corps*, and having also instigated to war, and armed, the Indian tribes, over which they had influence, had brought on themselves this act of retaliation. Mr. Johnston also had engaged actively in the war against the United States.

The schooner was at the foot of the rapids; the Americans had run her down, but she grounded on a ledge of rocks, whence they could not dislodge her, and so they had burnt her to the water's edge.

Le Saut de Ste. Marie, or as it is shortly called, *Saut Ste. Marie*, is a rapid at the outlet of Lake Superior, and may be five hundred or six hundred yards wide; its length may be estimated at three quarters of a mile, and the descent of the water at about twenty feet. At the lower extremity the river widens to about a mile, and here there are a certain number of houses. The north bank belongs to Great Britain; the southern to the United States. It was on the American side that Mr. Johnston lived. Before the war he was collector of the port for the American government. On the same side resided a Mr. Nolin, with his family, consisting of three half-breed boys and as many girls, one of whom was passably pretty. He was an old Indian trader, and his house and furniture showed signs of his former prosperity. On the British side we found

Mr. Charles Ermatinger, who had a pretty establishment: he dwelt temporarily in a house that belonged to Nolin, but he was building another of stone, very elegant, and had just finished a grist mill. He thought that the last would lead the inhabitants to sow more grain than they did. These inhabitants are principally old Canadian boatmen, married to half-breed or Indian women. The fish afford them subsistence during the greater part of the year, and provided they secure potatoes enough to carry them through the remainder, they are content. It is to be regretted that these people are not more industrious, for the land is very fertile.

On the 1st of August, an express was sent to *Michilimackinac* (Mackinaw) to inform the commandant thereof what had happened at *Saut Ste Marie*. While expecting the return of the messenger, we put ourselves in a state of defence, in case that by chance the Americans should make another irruption. The thing was not improbable, for according to some expressions which fell from one of their number who spoke French, their objects was to capture the furs of the Northwest Company, which were expected to arrive shortly from the interior. We invited some Indians, who were camped on *Pine Point*, at some distance from the *Saut*, to help us in case of need; which they promised to do. Meanwhile we had no provisions, as everything had been carried off by the American forces, and were obliged to subsist on such brook trout as we could take with hook and line, and on wild raspberries.

On the 4th, the express returned, without having been able to accomplish his mission: he had found the island of Mackinaw so completely blockaded by the enemy, that it was impossible to reach it, without running the greatest risk of being made prisoner.

On the 12th, we heard distinctly the discharges of artillery which our people were firing off at Michilimackinac, although the distance was nearly sixty miles. We thought it was an attempt of the enemy to retake that post, but we afterward learned that it was only a royal salute in honor of the birthday of the prince regent. We learned, however, during our stay at Saut Ste. Marie, that the Americans had really made a descent upon the island, but were compelled to retire with a considerable loss.

On the 19th, some of the partners arrived from Fort William, preceding the flotilla which was coming down richly laden with furs. They sent on Mr. Decoigne in a light canoe, with letters to Montreal, to order provisions to meet this brigade.

On the 21st, the canoe on which I was a passenger, was sent to the mouth of *French* river, to observe the motions of the enemy. The route lay between a range of low islands, and a shelvy beach, very monotonous and dreary. We remained at the entrance of the aforesaid river till the 25th, when the fleet of loaded canoes, forty-seven in number, arrived there. The value of the furs which they carried could not be estimated at less than a million of dollars: an important prize for the Americans, if they could have laid their hands upon it. We were three hundred and thirty-five men, all well armed; a large camp was formed, with a breast-work of fur-packs, and we kept watch all night. The next morning we began to ascend French river, and were soon out of reach of the dreaded foe. French river flows from the N. E. and empties into Lake Huron, about one hundred and twenty miles from Saut Ste. Marie. We reached Lake Nipissing, of which it is the outlet, the same evening, and encamped. We crossed that lake on the 27th, made a number of portages, and encamped again, not far from *Mattawan.*

On the 28th we entered, at an early hour, the river *Ottawa*, and encamped, in the evening, at the *Portage des deux Joachims.* This is a grand river, but obstructed by many falls and rapids on its way to join the St. Lawrence; which caused us to make many portages, and so we arrived on the 31st at *Kettle falls.*

The rock which here arrests the course of the *Ottawa*, extends from shore to shore, and so completely cuts off the waters, that at the time we passed none was seen falling over, but sinking by subterranean channels, or fissures in the rock, it boiled up below, from seven or eight different openings, not unlike water in a huge caldron, whence the first explorers of the country gave it the name of *Chaudière* or Caldron falls. Mr. P. Wright resided in this place, where he had a fine establishment and a great number of men employed in cultivating the land, and getting out lumber.

We left the *Chaudières* a little before sunset, and passed very soon the confluence of the *Rideau* or *Curtain river*. This river, which casts itself into the Ottawa over a rock twenty-five by thirty feet high, is divided in the middle of the fall by a little island, which parts the waters into two white sheets, resembling a double curtain open in the middle and spreading out below. The *coup d'œil* is really picturesque; the rays of the setting sun, which struck the waters obliquely as we passed, heightened exceedingly their beauty, and rendered it worthy of a pencil more skilful than mine.

We voyaged till midnight, when we stopped to

let our men take a little repose. This rest was only for two hours. At sunrise on the 1st September, we reached *Long-Saut*, where, having procured guides, we passed that dangerous rapid, and set foot on shore near the dwelling-house of a Mr. M'Donell, who sent us milk and fruits for our breakfast. Toward noon we passed the lake of the Two Mountains, where I began to see the mountain of my native isle. About two o'clock, we passed the rapids of St. Ann.* Soon after we came opposite *Saut St. Louis* and the village of *Caughnawaga*, passed that last rapid of so many, and landed at Montreal, a little before sunset.

I hastened to the paternal roof, where the family were not less surprised than overjoyed at beholding me. Not having heard of me, since I had sailed from New York, they had believed, in

* "Far-famed and so well described," adds Mr. Franchere, in his own translation, but I prefer to leave the expression in its original striking simplicity, as he wrote it before he had heard of MOORE. Every reader remembers:—

"Soon as the woods on shore grow dim,
We'll sing at St. Ann's our parting hymn."

Canadian Boatman's Song.

accordance with the common report, that I had been murdered by the savages, with Mr. M'Kay and the crew of the Tonquin: and certainly, it was by the goodness of Providence that I found myself thus safe and sound, in the midst of my relations and friends, at the end of a voyage accompanied by so many perils, and in which so many of my companions had met with an untimely death.

CHAPTER XXIX.

Present State of the Countries visited by the Author.—Correction of Mr. Irving's Statements respecting St. Louis.

THE last chapter closes the original French narrative of my travels around and across the continent, as published thirty-three years ago. The translation follows that narrative as exactly as possible, varying from it only in the correction of a few not very important errors of fact. It speaks of places and persons as I spoke of them then. I would not willingly lose the verisimilitude of this natural and unadorned description, in order to indulge in any new turns of style or more philosophical reflections.

But since that period many changes have occurred in the scenes which I so long ago visited and described. Though they are well known, I may be pardoned for alluding to them.

The natives of the Sandwich islands, who were in a state of paganism at that time, have since adopted a form of Christianity, have made considerable progress in imitating the civilization of Europe, and even, at this moment, begin to entertain the idea of annexation to the United States. It appears, however, that the real natives are rapidly dwindling away by the effects of their vices, which an exotic and ill-assimilated civilization has rather increased than diminished, and to which religion has not succeeded in applying a remedy.

At the mouth of the Columbia, whole tribes, and among them, the *Clatsops*, have been swept away by disease. Here again, licentious habits universally diffused, spread a fatal disorder through the whole nation, and undermining the constitutions of all, left them an easy prey to the first contagion or epidemic sickness. But missionaries of various Christian sects have labored among the Indians of the Columbia also; not to speak of the missions of the Catholic Church, so well known by the narrative of Father De Smet and others; and numbers have been taught to cultivate the soil, and thus to provide against the famines to which they were formerly exposed from their dependence on the precarious resources of the chase; while others have received, in the faith of Christ, the true principle of national permanence, and a living germ of civilization, which may afterward be developed.

Emigration has also carried to the Oregon the axe of the settler, as well as the canoe and pack of the fur-trader. The fertile valleys and prairies of the Willamet—once the resort of the deer, the elk, and the antelope, are now tilled by the industrious husbandman. Oregon City, so near old "Astoria," whose first log fort I saw and described, is now an Archiepiscopal see, and the capital of a territory, which must soon be a state of the Union.

Of the regions east of the mountains described in my itinerary, little can be said in respect to improvement: they remain in the same wild state. The interest of the Hudson's Bay Company, as an association of fur-traders, is opposed to agricultural improvements, whose operation would be to drive off and extinguish the wild animals that furnish their commerce with its object. But on Lake Superior steamboats have supplanted the birch-bark canoe of the Indian and the fur-trader, and at Saut Ste. Marie, especially on the American side, there is now every sign of prosperity. How remote and wild was the region beyond, through which I passed, may be estimated by the fact that in thirty-eight years the onward-rolling wave of our population has but just reached its confines.

Canada, although it has not kept pace with the United States, has yet wonderfully advanced in forty years. The valley of the Ottawa, that great artery of the St. Lawrence, where I thought it worth while to notice the residence of an enterprising farmer and lumber merchant, is now a populous district, well cultivated, and sprinkled with villages, towns, and cities.

The reader, in perusing my first chapter, found a description of the city of New York in 1810, and of the neighboring village of Brooklyn. It would be superfluous to establish a comparison at this day. At that time, it will be observed, the mere breaking out of war between America and England was thought to involve the sacrifice of an American commercial establishment on the Pacific, on the ground of its supplies being necessarily cut off (it was supposed), and of the United States government being unable to protect it from hostile attack. At present it suffices to remark that while New York, then so inconsiderable a port, is now perhaps the third city in the world, the United States also, are, undoubtedly, a first-rate power, unassailable at home, and formidable abroad, to the greatest nations.

As in my preface I alluded to Mr. Irving's "Astoria," as reflecting, in my opinion, unjustly, upon the young men engaged in the first expedition to the mouth of the Columbia, it may suffice here to observe, without entering into particulars, that my narrative, which I think answers for its own fidelity, clearly shows that some of them, at least did not want courage, activity, zeal for the interests of the company, while it existed, and patient endurance of hardship. And although it forms no part of the narrative or my voyage, yet as subsequent visits to the West and an intimate knowledge of St. Louis, enable me to correct Mr. Irving's poetical rather than accurate description of that place, I may well do it here. St. Louis now bids fair to rival ere long the "Queen of the West;" Mr. Irving describes her as a small trading place, where trappers, half-breeds, gay, frivolous Canadian boatmen, &c., &c., congregated and revelled, with that lightness and buoyancy of spirit inherited from their French forefathers; the indolent Creole of St. Louis caring for little more than the enjoyment of the present hour; a motley population, half-civilized, half-barbarous, thrown, on his canvas, into one general, confused (I allow highly *picturesque*) mass, without respect of persons: but it is fair to say, with due homage to the talent of the sketcher, who has verged slightly on caricature in the use of that humor-loving pencil admired by all the world, that St. Louis even then contained its noble, industrious, and I may say, princely merchants; it could boast its *Chouteaus*, *Soulands*, *Céré*, *Chéniers*, *Vallées*, and *La Croix*, with other kindred spirits, whose descendants prove the worth of their sires by their own, and are now among the leading business men, as their fathers were the pioneers, of the flourishing St. Louis.

With these remarks, which I make simply as an act of justice in connection with the general subject of the founding of "Astoria," but in which I mean to convey no imputation on the intentional fairness of the accomplished author to whom I have alluded, I take a respectful leave of my readers.

APPENDIX.*

In Chapter XVII. I promised the reader to give him an account of the fate of some of the persons who left Astoria before, and after its sale or transfer to the British. I will now redeem that pledge.

Messrs. Ramsay Crooks, R. M'Lelland, and Robert Stuart, after enduring all sorts of fatigue, dangers and hair-breadth escapes with their lives —all which have been so graphically described by Washington Irving in his "Astoria," finally reached St. Louis and New York.

Mr. Clapp went to the Marquesas Islands, where he entered into the service of his country

* We have thought it best to give this Appendix, excepting some abbreviations rendered necessary to avoid repetition of what has been stated before, in Mr. Franchere's own words, particularly as a specimen of his own English style may be justly interesting to the reader.

in the capacity of Midshipman under Commodore Porter—made his escape from there in company with Lieutenant Gamble of the Marine corps, by directions of the Commodore, was captured by the British, landed at Buenos Ayres, and finally reached New York.

D. M'Dougall, as a reward for betraying the trust reposed in him by Mr. Astor, was made a Partner of the Northwest Company, crossed the mountains, and died a miserable death at *Bas de la Rivière*, Winipeg. Donald M'Kenzie, his co-adjutor, went back to the Columbia River, where he amassed a considerable fortune, with which he retired, and lived in Chautauque County in this state, where he died a few years since unknown and neglected:—he was a very selfish man, who cared for no one but himself.

It remains only to speak of Messrs. J. C. Halsey, Russell, Farnham, and Alfred Seton, who, it will be remembered, embarked with Mr. Hunt on the "Pedlar," in Feb. 1814.

Leaving the River about the 1st of April, they proceeded to the Russian establishment at Sitka,

Norfolk Sound, where they fell in with two or three more American vessels, which had come to trade with the natives or to avoid the British cruisers. While there, a sail under British colors appeared, and Mr. Hunt sent Mr. Seton to ascertain who she was. She turned out to be the "Forester," Captain Pigott, a repeating signal ship and letter-of-marque, sent from England in company of a fleet intended for the South Seas. On further acquaintance with the captain, Mr. Seton (from whom I derive these particulars) learned a fact which has never before been published, and which will show the solicitude and perseverance of Mr. ASTOR. After despatching the "Lark" from New York, fearing that she might be intercepted by the British, he sent orders to his correspondent in England to purchase and fit out a British bottom, and despatch her to the Columbia to relieve the establishment.

When Mr. Hunt learned this fact, he determined to leave Mr. Halsey at Sitka, and proceeding himself northward, landed Mr. Farnham on the coast of *Kamskatka*, to go over land with despatches for Mr. Astor. Mr. Farnham accomplished the journey, reached Hamburg, whence he sailed for the West Indies, and finally arrived at New York, having made the entire circuit of the globe.

The "Pedlar" then sailed to the southeast, and soon reached the coast of California, which she approached to get a supply of provisions. Nearing one of the harbors, they descried a vessel at anchor inside, showing American colors. Hauling their wind, they soon came close to the stranger, which, to their surprise, turned out to be the Spanish corvette "Santa Barbara," which sent boats alongside the "Pedlar," and captured her, and kept possession of the prize for some two months, during which they dropped down to *San Blas*. Here Mr. Hunt proposed to Mr. Seton to cross the continent and reach the United States the best way he could. Mr. Seton, accordingly, went to the Isthmus of Darien, where he was detained several months by sickness, but finally reached Carthagena, where a British fleet was lying in the roads, to take off the English merchants, who in consequence of the revolutionary movements going on, sought shelter under their own flag. Here Mr. Seton, reduced to the last stage of destitution and squalor, boldly applied to Captain Bentham, the commander of the squadron, who, finding him to be a gentleman, offered him every needful assistance, gave him a berth in his own cabin, and finally landed him safely on the Island of Jamaica, whence he, too, found his way to New York.

Of all those engaged in the expedition there are now but four survivors—Ramsay Crooks, Esq. the late President of the American Fur Company; Alfred Seton, Esq., Vice-president of the Sun Mutual Insurance Company; both of New York city; Benjamin Pillet of Canada; and the author, living also in New York. All the rest have paid the debt of nature, but their names are recorded in the foregoing pages.

Notwithstanding the illiberal remarks made by Captain Thorn on the persons who were on board the ill-fated Tonquin, and reproduced by Mr. Irving in his "Astoria"—these young men who were represented as "Bar keepers or Billiard markers, most of whom had fled from Justice, &c."—I feel it a duty to say that they were for the most part, of good parentage, liberal education and every way were qualified to discharge the duties of their respective stations. The remarks on the general character of the voyageurs employed as boat-men and Mechanics, and the attempt to cast ridicule on their "Braggart and swaggering manners" come with a bad grace from the author of "Astoria," when we consider that in that very work Mr. Irving is compelled to admit their indomitable energy, their fidelity to their employers, and their cheerfulness under the most trying circumstances in which men can be placed.

With respect to Captain Thorn, I must confess that though a stern commander and an irritable man, he paid the strictest attention to the health of his crew. His complaints of the squalid appearance of the Canadians and mechanics who were on board, can be abated of their force by giving a description of the accommodation of these people. The Tonquin was a small ship; its forecastle was destined for the crew performing duty before the mast. The room allotted for the accommodation of the twenty men destined for the establishment, was abaft the forecastle; a bulk-head had been let across, and a door led from the forecastle into a dark, unventilated, unwholesome place, where they were all heaped together, without means of locomotion, and consequently deprived of that exercise of the body so necessary to health. Add to that, we had no physician on board. In view of these facts, can the complaints of the gallant Captain be sustained? Of course Mr. Irving was ignorant of these circumstances, as well as of many others which he might have known, had some one suggested to him to ask a few questions of persons who were within his reach at the time of his publication. I have (I need scarcely say) no personal animosity against the unfortunate Captain; he always treated me, individually, as well as I could expect; and if, in the course of my narrative, I have been severe on his actions, I was impelled by a sense of justice to my friends on board, as well as by the circumstance that such explanations of his general deportment were requisite to convey the historical truth to my readers.

The idea of a conspiracy against him on board is so absurd that it really does not deserve notice. The threat, or rather the proposal made to him by Mr. M'Kay, in the following words—"if you say fight, fight it is"—originated in a case where one of the sailors had maltreated a Canadian lad, who came to complain to Mr. M'Kay. The captain would not interpose his authority, and said in my presence, "Let them fight out their own battles:"—it was upon that answer that Mr. M'Kay gave vent to the expression quoted above. I might go on with a long list of inaccuracies, more or less grave or trivial, in the beautifully written work of Mr. Irving, but it would be tedious to go through the whole of them. The few remarks to which I have given place above, will suffice to prove that the assertion made in the preface was not unwarranted. It is far from my intention to enter the lists with a man of the literary merit and reputation of Mr. Irving, but as a narrator of events of which I was an EYE-WITNESS, I felt bound to tell the truth, although that truth might impugn the historical accuracy of a work which ranks as a classic in the language. At the same time I entirely exonerate Mr. Irving from any intention of prejudicing the minds of his readers, as he doubtless had only in view to support the character of his friend: that sentiment is worthy of a generous heart, but it should not be gratified, nor would he wish to gratify it, I am sure, at the expense of the character of others.

NOTE BY THE EDITOR.

Perhaps even contrary to the wish of Mr. Franchere, I have left the above almost word for word as he wrote it. It is a part of the history of the affairs related as well in Mr. Irving's ASTORIA as in the present volume, that the reclamations of one of the clerks on that famous and unfortunate voyage of the Tonquin, against the disparaging description of himself and his colleagues given in the former work, should be fairly recorded. At the same time, I can not help stating my own impression that a natural susceptibility, roused by those slighting remarks from Captain Thorn's correspondence, to which Mr. Irving as an historian gives currency, has somewhat blinded my excellent friend to the tone of banter, so characteristic of the chronicler of the Knickerbockers, in which all these particulars are given, more as traits of the character of the stern old sea-captain, with his hearty contempt for land-lubbers and literary clerks, than as a dependable account of the persons on board his ship, some of whom might have been, and as we see by the present work, were, in fact, very meritorious characters, for whose literary turn, and faithful journalizing (which seems to have especially provoked the captain's wrath), now at the end of more than forty years, we have so much reason to be thankful. Certainly Mr. Irving himself, who has drawn frequently on Mr. Franchere's narrative, could not, from his well-known taste in such matters, be insensible to the Defoe-like simplicity thereof, nor to the picturesque descriptions, worthy of a professional pen, with which it is sprinkled.

THE END.

J. S. REDFIELD,

110 AND 112 NASSAU STREET, NEW YORK,

HAS JUST PUBLISHED:

EPISODES OF INSECT LIFE.

By Acheta Domestica. In Three Series: I. Insects of Spring.—II. Insects of Summer.—III. Insects of Autumn. Beautifully illustrated. Crown 8vo., cloth, gilt, price $2.00 each. The same beautifully colored after nature, extra gilt, $4.00 each.

"A book elegant enough for the centre table, witty enough for after dinner, and wise enough for the study and the school-room. One of the beautiful lessons of this work is the kindly view it takes of nature. Nothing is made in vain not only, but nothing is made ugly or repulsive. A charm is thrown around every object, and life suffused through all, suggestive of the Creator's goodness and wisdom."—*N. Y. Evangelist.*

"Moths, glow-worms, lady-birds, May-flies, bees, and a variety of other inhabitants of the insect world, are descanted upon in a pleasing style, combining scientific information with romance, in a manner peculiarly attractive."—*Commercial Advertiser.*

"The book includes solid instruction as well as genial and captivating mirth. The scientific knowledge of the writer is thoroughly reliable."—*Examiner*

MEN AND WOMEN OF THE EIGHTEENTH CENTURY.

By Arsene Houssaye, with beautifully Engraved Portraits of Louis XV., and Madame de Pompadour. Two volume 12mo. 450 pages each, extra superfine paper, price $2.50.

Contents.—Dufresny, Fontenelle, Marivaux, Piron, The Abbé Prevost, Gentil-Bernard, Florian, Boufflers, Diderot, Grétry, Riverol, Louis XV., Greuze, Boucher, The Vanloos, Lantara, Watteau, La Motte, Dehle, Abbé Trublet, Buffon, Dorat, Cardinal de Bernis, Crébillon the Gay, Marie Antoinette, Made. de Pompadour, Vadé, Mlle. Camargo, Mlle. Clairon, Mad. de la Popelinière, Sophie Arnould, Crébillon the Tragic, Mlle. Guimard, Three Pages in the Life of Dancourt, A Promenade in the Palais-Royal, the Chevalier de la Clos.

"A more fascinating book than this rarely issues from the teeming press. Fascinating in its subject; fascinating in its style: fascinating in its power to lead the reader into castle-building of the most gorgeous and bewitching description."—*Courier & Enquirer.*

"This is a most welcome book, full of information and amusement, in the form of memoirs, comments, and anecdotes. It has the style of light literature, with the usefulness of the gravest. It should be in every library, and the hands of every reader." *Boston Commonwealth.*

"A Book of Books.—Two deliciously spicy volumes, that are a perfect *bonne bouche* for an epicure in reading."—*Home Journal.*

PHILOSOPHERS AND ACTRESSES

By ARSENE HOUSSAYE. With beautifully-engraved Portraits of Voltaire and Mad. Parabère. Two vols., 12mo, price $2.50.

"We have here the most charming book we have read these many days,—so powerful in its fascination that we have been held for hours from our imperious labors, or needful slumbers, by the entrancing influence of its pages. One of the most desirable fruits of the prolific field of literature of the present season."—*Portland Eclectic.*

"Two brilliant and fascinating—we had almost said, bewitching—volumes, combining information and amusement, the lightest gossip, with solid and serviceable wisdom."—*Yankee Blade.*

"It is a most admirable book, full of originality, wit, information and philosophy Indeed, the vividness of the book is extraordinary. The scenes and descriptions are absolutely life-like."—*Southern Literary Gazette.*

"The works of the present writer are the only ones the spirit of whose rhetoric does justice to those times, and in fascination of description and style equal the fascinations they descant upon."—*New Orleans Commercial Bulletin.*

"The author is a brilliant writer, and serves up his sketches in a sparkling manner" *Christian Freeman.*

ANCIENT EGYPT UNDER THE PHARAOHS.

By JOHN KENDRICK, M. A. In 2 vols., 12mo, price $2.50.

"No work has heretofore appeared suited to the wants of the historical student, which combined the labors of artists, travellers, interpreters and critics, during the periods from the earliest records of the monarchy to its final absorption in the empire of Alexander. This work supplies this deficiency."—*Olive Branch.*

"Not only the geography and political history of Egypt under the Pharaohs are given, but we are furnished with a minute account of the domestic manners and customs of the inhabitants, their language, laws, science, religion, agriculture, navigation and commerce."—*Commercial Advertiser.*

"These volumes present a comprehensive view of the results of the combined labors of travellers, artists, and scientific explorers, which have effected so much during the present century toward the development of Egyptian archæology and history."—*Journal of Commerce.*

"The descriptions are very vivid and one wanders, delighted with the author, through the land of Egypt, gathering at every step, new phases of her wondrous history, and ends with a more intelligent knowledge than he ever before had, of the land of the Pharaohs."—*American Spectator.*

COMPARATIVE PHYSIOGNOMY;

Or Resemblances between Men and Animals. By J. W. REDFIELD, M. D. In one vol., 8vo, with several hundred illustrations. price, $2.00.

"Dr. Redfield has produced a very curious, amusing, and instructive book, curious in its originality and illustrations, amusing in the comparisons and analyses, and instructive because it contains very much useful information on a too much neglected subject. It will be eagerly read and quickly appreciated."—*National Ægis.*

"The whole work exhibits a good deal of scientific research, intelligent observation, and ingenuity."—*Daily Union.*

"Highly entertaining even to those who have little time to study the science."—*Detroit Daily Advertiser.*

"This is a remarkable volume and will be read by two classes, those who study for information, and those who read for amusement. For its originality and entertaining character, we commend it to our readers."—*Albany Express.*

"It is overflowing with wit, humor, and originality, and profusely illustrated. The whole work is distinguished by vast research and knowledge."—*Knickerbocker.*

"The plan is a novel one; the proofs striking, and must challenge the attention of the curious."—*Daily Advertiser*

NOTES AND EMENDATIONS OF SHAKESPEARE.

Notes and Emendations to the Text of Shakespeare's Plays, from the Early Manuscript Corrections in a copy of the folio of 1632, in the possession of JOHN PAYNE COLLIER, Esq., F.S.A. Third edition, with a fac-simile of the Manuscript Corrections. 1 vol 12mo, cloth, $1 50.

"It is not for a moment to be doubted, we think, that in this volume a contribution has been made to the clearness and accuracy of Shakespeare's text, by far the most important of any offered or attempted since Shakespeare lived and wrote."—*Lond. Exam*

"The corrections which Mr. Collier has here given to the world are, we venture to think, of more value than the labors of nearly all the critics on Shakespeare's text put together."—*London Literary Gazette.*

"It is a rare gem in the history of literature, and can not fail to command the attention of all the amateurs of the writings of the immortal dramatic poet."—*Ch'ston Cour*

"It is a book absolutely indispensable to every admirer of Shakespeare who wishes to read him understandingly."—*Louisville Courier.*

"It is clear from internal evidence, that for the most part they are genuine restorations of the original plays. They carry conviction with them."—*Home Journal.*

"This volume is an almost indispensable companion to any of the editions of Shakespeare, so numerous and often important are many of the corrections."—*Register Philadelphia.*

THE HISTORY OF THE CRUSADES.

By JOSEPH FRANÇOIS MICHAUD. Translated by W. Robson, 3 vols. 12mo., maps, $3 75.

"It is comprehensive and accurate in the detail of facts, methodical and lucid in arrangement, with a lively and flowing narrative."—*Journal of Commerce.*

"We need not say that the work of Michaud has superseded all other histories of the Crusades. This history has long been the standard work with all who could read it in its original language. Another work on the same subject is as improbable as a new history of the 'Decline and Fall of the Roman Empire.'"—*Salem Freeman.*

"The most faithful and masterly history ever written of the wild wars for the Holy Land."—*Philadelphia American Courier.*

"The ability, diligence, and faithfulness, with which Michaud has executed his great task, are undisputed; and it is to his well-filled volumes that the historical student must now resort for copious and authentic facts, and luminous views respecting this most romantic and wonderful period in the annals of the Old World."—*Boston Daily Courier.*

MARMADUKE WYVIL.

An Historical Romance of 1651, by HENRY W. HERBERT, author of the "Cavaliers of England," &c., &c. Fourteenth Edition. Revised and Corrected.

"This is one of the best works of the kind we have ever read—full of thrilling incidents and adventures in the stirring times of Cromwell, and in that style which has made the works of Mr. Herbert so popular."—*Christian Freeman, Boston.*

"The work is distinguished by the same historical knowledge, thrilling incident, and pictorial beauty of style, which have characterized all Mr. Herbert's fictions and imparted to them such a bewitching interest."—*Yankee Blade.*

"The author out of a simple plot and very few characters, has constructed a novel of deep interest and of considerable historical value. It will be found well worth reading"—*National Ægis, Worcester.*

SKETCHES OF THE IRISH BAR.

By the Right Hon. RICHARD LALOR SHEIL, M. P. Edited with a Memoir and Notes, by Dr. SHELTON MACKENZIE. Fourth Edition. In 2 vols. Price $2 00.

"They attracted universal attention by their brilliant and pointed style, and their liberality of sentiment. The Notes embody a great amount of biographical information, literary gossip, legal and political anecdote, and amusing reminiscences, and, in fact, omit nothing that is essential to the perfect elucidation of the text."—*New York Tribune.*

"They are the best edited books we have met for many a year. They form, with Mackenzie's notes, a complete biographical dictionary, containing succinct and clever sketches of all the famous people of England, and particularly of Ireland, to whom the slightest allusions are made in the text."—*The Citizen (John Mitchel).*

"Dr. Mackenzie deserves the thanks of men of letters, particularly of Irishmen, for his research and care. Altogether, the work is one we can recommend in the highest terms."—*Philadelphia City Item.*

"Such a repertory of wit, humor, anecdote, and out-gushing fun, mingled with the deepest pathos, when we reflect upon the sad fate of Ireland, as this book affords, it were hard to find written in any other pair of covers."—*Buffalo Daily Courier.*

"As a whole, a more sparkling lively series of portraits was hardly ever set in a single gallery It is Irish all over; the wit, the folly, the extravagance, and the fire are all alike characteristic of writer and subjects."—*New York Evangelist.*

"These volumes afford a rich treat to the lovers of literature."—*Hartford Christian Sec.*

CLASSIC AND HISTORIC PORTRAITS.

By JAMES BRUCE. 12mo, cloth, $1 00.

"A series of personal sketches of distinguished individuals of all ages, embracing pen and ink portraits of near sixty persons from Sappho down to Madame de Stael. They show much research, and possess that interest which attaches to the private life of those whose names are known to fame."—*New Haven Journal and Courier.*

"They are comprehensive, well-written, and judicious, both in the selection of subjects and the manner of treating them."—*Boston Atlas.*

"The author has painted in minute touches the characteristics of each with various personal details, all interesting, and all calculated to furnish to the mind's eye a complete portraiture of the individual described."—*Albany Knickerbocker.*

"The sketches are full and graphic, many authorities having evidently been consulted by the author in their preparation."—*Boston Journal.*

THE WORKINGMAN'S WAY IN THE WORLD.

Being the Autobiography of a Journeyman Printer. By CHARLES MANBY SMITH, author of "Curiosities of London Life." 12mo, cloth, $1 00.

"Written by a man of genius and of most extraordinary powers of description."—*Boston Traveller.*

"It will be read with no small degree of interest by the professional brethren of the author, as well as by all who find attractions in a well-told tale of a workingman."—*Boston Atlas.*

"An amusing as well as instructive book, telling how humble obscurity cuts its way through the world with energy, perseverance, and integrity."—*Albany Knickerbocker.*

"The book is the most entertaining we have met with for months."—*Philadelphia Evening Bulletin.*

"He has evidently moved through the world with his eyes open and having a vein of humor in his nature, has written one of the most readable books of the season"—*Zion's Herald.*

MACAULAY'S SPEECHES.

Speeches by the Right Hon. T. B. MACAULAY, M. P., Author of "The History of England," "Lays of Ancient Rome," &c., &c. Two vols., 12mo, price $2.00.

"It is hard to say whether his poetry, his speeches in parliament, or his brilliant essays, are the most charming; each has raised him to very great eminence, and would be sufficient to constitute the reputation of any ordinary man."—*Sir Archibald Alison*

"It may be said that Great Britain has produced no statesman since Burke, who has united in so eminent a degree as Macaulay the lofty and cultivated genius, the eloquent orator, and the sagacious and far-reaching politician."—*Albany Argus.*

"We do not know of any living English orator, whose eloquence comes so near the ancient ideal—close, rapid, powerful, *practical* reasoning, animated by an intense earnestness of feeling."—*Courier & Enquirer.*

"Mr. Macaulay has lately acquired as great a reputation as an orator, as he had formerly won as an essayist and historian. He takes in his speeches the same wide and comprehensive grasp of his subject that he does in his essays, and treats it in the same elegant style."—*Philadelphia Evening Bulletin.*

"The same elaborate finish, sparkling antithesis, full sweep and copious flow of thought, and transparency of style, which made his essays so attractive, are found in his speeches. They are so perspicuous, so brilliantly studded with ornament and illustration, and so resistless in their current, that they appear at the time to be the wisest and greatest of human compositions."—*New York Evangelist.*

TRENCH ON PROVERBS.

On the Lessons in Proverbs, by RICHARD CHENEVIX TRENCH, B. D., Professor of Divinity in King's College, London, Author of the "Study of Words." 12mo, cloth, 50 cents.

"Another charming book by the author of the "Study of Words," on a subject which is so ingeniously treated, that we wonder no one has treated it before."—*Yankee Blade.*

"It is a book at once profoundly instructive, and at the same time deprived of all approach to dryness, by the charming manner in which the subject is treated."—*Arthur's Home Gazette.*

"It is a wide field, and one which the author has well cultivated, adding not only to his own reputation, but a valuable work to our literature."—*Albany Evening Transcript.*

"The work shows an acute perception, a genial appreciation of wit, and great research. It is a very rare and agreeable production, which may be read with profit and delight."—*New York Evangelist.*

"The style of the author is terse and vigorous—almost a model in its kind."—*Portland Eclectic.*

THE LION SKIN

And the Lover Hunt; by CHARLES DE BERNARD. 12mo, $1.00.

"It is not often the novel-reader can find on his bookseller's shelf a publication so full of incidents and good humor, and at the same time so provocative of honest thought."—*National* (Worcester, Mass.) *Ægis.*

"It is full of incidents; and the reader becomes so interested in the principal personages in the work, that he is unwilling to lay the book down until he has learned their whole history."—*Boston Olive Branch.*

"It is refreshing to meet occasionally with a well-published story which is written for a story, and for nothing else—which is not tipped with the snapper of a moral, or loaded in the handle with a pound of philanthropy, or an equal quantity of leaden philosophy."—*Springfield Republican.*

MOORE'S LIFE OF SHERIDAN.

Memoirs of the Life of the Rt. Hon. Richard Brinsley Sheridan, by THOMAS MOORE, with Portrait after Sir Joshua Reynolds. Two vols., 12mo, cloth, $2.00.

"One of the most brilliant biographies in English literature. It is the life of a wit written by a wit, and few of Tom Moore's most sparkling poems are more brilliant and fascinating than this biography."—*Boston Transcript.*

"This is at once a most valuable biography of the most celebrated wit of the times, and one of the most entertaining works of its gifted author."—*Springfield Republican.*

"The Life of Sheridan, the wit, contains as much food for serious thought as the best sermon that was ever penned."—*Arthur's Home Gazette.*

"The sketch of such a character and career as Sheridan's by such hand as Moore's, can never cease to be attractive."—*N. Y. Courier and Enquirer.*

"The work is instructive and full of interest."—*Christian Intelligencer.*

"It is a gem of biography; full of incident, elegantly written, warmly appreciative, and on the whole candid and just. Sheridan was a rare and wonderful genius, and has in this work justice done to his surpassing merits."—*N. Y. Evangelist.*

BARRINGTON'S SKETCHES.

Personal Sketches of his own Time, by SIR JONAH BARRINGTON, Judge of the High Court of Admiralty in Ireland, with Illustrations by Darley. Third Edition, 12mo, cloth, $1 25.

"A more entertaining book than this is not often thrown in our way. His sketches of character are inimitable; and many of the prominent men of his time are hit off in the most striking and graceful outline."—*Albany Argus.*

"He was a very shrewd observer and eccentric writer, and his narrative of his own life, and sketches of society in Ireland during his times, are exceedingly humorous and interesting."—*N. Y. Commercial Advertiser.*

"It is one of those works which are conceived and written in so hearty a view, and brings before the reader so many palpable and amusing characters, that the entertainment and information are equally balanced."—*Boston Transcript.*

"This is one of the most entertaining books of the season."—*N. Y. Recorder.*

"It portrays in life-like colors the characters and daily habits of nearly all the English and Irish celebrities of that period."—*N. Y. Courier and Enquirer.*

JOMINI'S CAMPAIGN OF WATERLOO.

The Political and Military History of the Campaign of Waterloo from the French of Gen. Baron Jomini, by Lieut. S. V. BENET U. S. Ordnance, with a Map, 12mo, cloth, 75 cents.

"Of great value, both for its historical merit and its acknowledged impartiality."—*Christian Freeman, Boston.*

"It has long been regarded in Europe as a work of more than ordinary merit, while to military men his review of the tactics and manœuvres of the French Emperor during the few days which preceded his final and most disastrous defeat, is considered as instructive, as it is interesting."—*Arthur's Home Gazette.*

"It is a standard authority and illustrates a subject of permanent interest. With military students, and historical inquirers, it will be a favorite reference, and for the general reader it possesses great value and interest."—*Boston Transcript.*

"It throws much light on often mooted points respecting Napoleon's military and political genius. The translation is one of much vigor."—*Boston Commonwealth.*

"It supplies an important chapter in the most interesting and eventful period of Napoleon's military career."—*Savannah Daily News.*

"It is ably written and skillfully translated."—*Yankee Blade.*

TURKEY AND RUSSIA.

The latest and best Works published.

A YEAR WITH THE TURKS:

Or, Sketches of Travel in the European and Asiatic Dominions of the Sultan. By Warington W. Smyth, M. A. With a colored Ethnological Map of the Empire. 12mo., cloth 75 cents. *Second Edition now ready.*

"Wallachia, the Danube, and other places now so prominent, are made familiar by the plain, easy style of our author, while a flood of light is shed upon the Turks as a people, their system of government, the policy of their rulers, and the whole internal arrangement of the Ottoman Empire."—*Phila. National Argus.*

"We advise all those who wish for clear information with regard to the condition of the Empire, and the various races that make up the population, to get this book and read it."—*Boston Commonwealth.*

"This is a plain and simple history of a region invested just now with peculiar interest. The geography of the country is minutely set down, the character, habits, idiosyncrasies of its inhabitants thoroughly portrayed, its resources, wealth and wants pointedly referred to, its government, laws and provisions clearly defined."—*Buffalo Express.*

"Mr. Smyth traveled in Turkey in the fall of last year, and his descriptions of the country are therefore more recent than can be obtained elsewhere."—*Troy Daily Times.*

"Mr. Smyth is just the right sort of man for a pleasant and useful traveling companion; good-humored, shrewd, intelligent, observant, and blessed with a good stock of common sense; and he has given us in this small volume a graphic, attractive and instructive account of what he saw and heard and experienced during twelve months of travel through the wide-spread dominions of Sultan Mahmoud."—*Boston Traveller.*

ALSO, THE THIRD EDITION OF

THE RUSSIAN SHORES OF THE BLACK SEA:

With a Voyage down the Volga, and a Tour through the Country of the Don Cossacks. By Laurence Oliphant, Author of a "Journey to Nepaul." From the Third London edition. 12mo., cloth, two maps and eighteen cuts. 75 cents.

Seven hundred copies of this work are advertised by one English Circulating Library.

"The volume is adorned by a number of wood-cuts and by two useful maps. It is a valuable contribution to our knowledge of Russia, and should be read by all who desire to be well informed."—*N. Y. Commercial Advertiser.*

"His book is full of exceedingly valuable information, and is written in an attractive style."—*Cincinnati Christian Herald.*

"Mr. Oliphant is a fluent, easy, companionable writer, who tells us a great deal we want to know, without a particle either of pedantry or bombast. This neat little book, with its maps and illustrations, will prove a most acceptable informant to the general reader, and at the same time prove highly entertaining."—*Boston Transcript.*

"Mr. Oliphant is an acute observer, a shrewd and intelligent man, a clear, vigorous and distinct writer, and his book embodies the best account of Southern Russia that has ever appeared. His account of Sebastopol will find many interested readers."—*Boston Atlas.*

"This book reminds us more of Stephen's delightful Incidents of Travel than any other book with which we are acquainted. It is an extremely interesting and valuable book."—*Boston Traveller.*

SIMMS' REVOLUTIONARY TALES.

UNIFORM SERIES.

New and entirely Revised Edition of WILLIAM GILMORE SIMMS' Romances of the Revolution, with Illustrations by DARLEY. Each complete in one vol., 12mo, cloth; price $1.25.

I. THE PARTISAN. **III. KATHARINE WALTON.** (In press.)
II. MELLICHAMPE. **IV. THE SCOUT.** (In press.)
V. WOODCRAFT. (In press.)

"The field of Revolutionary Romance was a rich one, and Mr. Simms has worked it admirably."—*Louisville Journal.*

"But few novelists of the age evince more power in the conception of a story, more artistic skill in its management, or more naturalness in the final *denouëment* than Mr. Simms."—*Mobile Daily Advertiser.*

"Not only *par excellence the* literary man of the South, but next to no romance writer in America."—*Albany Knickerbocker.*

"Simms is a popular writer, and his romances are highly creditable to American literature."—*Boston Olive Branch.*

"These books are replete with daring and thrilling adventures, principally drawn from history."—*Boston Christian Freeman.*

"We take pleasure in noticing another of the series which Redfield is presenting to the country of the brilliant productions of one of the very ablest of our American authors—of one indeed who, in his peculiar sphere, is inimitable. This volume is a continuation of 'The Partisan.'"—*Philadelphia American Courier.*

ALSO UNIFORM WITH THE ABOVE

THE YEMASSEE,

A Romance of South Carolina. By WM. GILMORE SIMMS. New and entirely Revised Edition, with Illustrations by DARLEY. 12mo, cloth; price $1.25.

"In interest, it is second to but few romances in the language; in power, it holds a high rank; in healthfulness of style, it furnishes an example worthy of emulation."—*Greene County Whig.*

SIMMS' POETICAL WORKS.

Poems: Descriptive, Dramatic, Legendary, and Contemplative. By WM. GILMORE SIMMS. With a portrait on steel. 2 vols., 12mo, cloth; price $2.50.

CONTENTS: Norman Maurice; a Tragedy.—Atalantis; a Tale of the Sea.—Tales and Traditions of the South.—The City of the Silent—Southern Passages and Pictures.—Historical and Dramatic Sketches.—Scripture Legends.—Francesca da Rimini, etc.

"We are glad to see the poems of our best Southern author collected in two handsome volumes. Here we have embalmed in graphic and melodious verse the scenic wonders and charms of the South; and this feature of the work alone gives it a permanent and special value. None can read 'Southern Passages and Pictures' without feeling that therein the poetic aspects, association, and sentiment of Southern life and scenery are vitally enshrined. 'Norman Maurice' is a dramatic poem of peculiar scope and unusual interest; and 'Atalantis,' a poem upon which some of the author's finest powers of thought and expression are richly lavished. None of our poets offer so great a variety of style or a more original choice of subjects."—*Boston Traveller.*

"His versification is fluent and mellifluous, yet not lacking in point of vigor when an energetic style is requisite to the subject."—*N. Y. Commercial Advertiser.*

"Mr. Simms ranks among the first poets of our country, and these well-printed volumes contain poetical productions of rare merit."—*Washington (D. C.) Star.*

www.ingramcontent.com/pod-product-compliance
Lightning Source LLC
LaVergne TN
LVHW020120110826
845151LV00001B/225

* 9 7 8 1 4 2 5 5 4 2 0 4 7 *